The Debatable Alliance

AN ESSAY IN ANGLO-AMERICAN RELATIONS

BY

CORAL BELL

Issued under the auspices of the
Royal Institute of International Affairs

OXFORD UNIVERSITY PRESS

LONDON　NEW YORK　TORONTO

1964

Oxford University Press, Amen House, London E.C.4

GLASGOW NEW YORK TORONTO MELBOURNE WELLINGTON
BOMBAY CALCUTTA MADRAS KARACHI LAHORE DACCA
CAPE TOWN SALISBURY NAIROBI IBADAN ACCRA
KUALA LUMPUR HONG KONG

Printed in Great Britain by
The Bowering Press, Plymouth

Contents

I

The Post-War Balance

The debate

EVIDENCE enough that the Anglo-American relationship is a debatable one may be found in the fact that it is debated, even at tedious length. Evidence that it is an alliance in any specific or bilateral sense might be harder to establish. All fifteen of the member-states of NATO, to be sure, are formally allies, and it is no doubt true, though not an officially defensible proposition, that some allies are more allied than others. But the claim that the relationship between Britain and America is of more significance, or better worth examining than, say, that between Norway and Turkey would have to look to other evidence than the formal words of treaties.

It might look to the debate itself. 'Debatable' has, of course, overtones that convey more than the existence of debate. 'Dubious', suggests the dictionary, 'questionable, uncertain, ambiguous, contested between two parties'. In the last fifteen years most of the sentiment that might seem to justify these adjectives has been felt on the British side of the relationship, and practically all the debate has been in Britain. This is not surprising: since the war America has in the nature of things loomed enormously larger on the British horizon than Britain has on the American horizon. Indeed one would perhaps have to go back to the pre-revolutionary period to find a time when Britain was as vital a factor in American destinies as America has been in British destinies since 1940. The intensity of the debate in Britain is an index of the real importance of the interests involved.

But one need not retreat to the eighteenth century to find a time when the relationship with Britain seemed to many Americans to raise the issues of national identity and purpose that some people in Britain have seen in the relation with America in the post-war period. There is a direct parallel between the pre-1917 debate over the U.S. entry into the first world war and the contemporary debate in Britain, which is essentially over the British role in the present power conflict. The progressive-pacifist movement in Woodrow Wilson's America and the CND— New Left group now in Britain have shared not only the repudiation of power as an instrument of diplomacy, and a tendency to see industrialists with markets to win as the sponsors of conflict, a preoccupation with social and economic reform and a belief that more weapons meant fewer benefits at home, but a kind of provincialism in a sense of the unique importance of their own nation's international role, as an example to the world both domestically and in foreign policy, a natural standard bearer to lead the powers towards its own righteousness.[1] It has been ironical but inevitable that the sector of British opinion for whom, throughout the nineteenth century, America seemed most unqualifiedly the good society, the young radical intelligentsia, should now be its most ardent critics. Once they saw America as the society that had rejected both the class hierarchy and power politics, the last best hope of earth. Now they tend to see it not only as the very fount and origin of power politics, but (swallowing Vance Packer's ingenuous conclusions), as domestically a rat-race for status-seekers. Isolationism is

---

[1] Cf. Aneurin Bevan's remark: 'There is only one hope for mankind, and that hope still remains in this little island.' Bevan did not of course share most CND positions. For the American side of this parallel see Arthur Link, *Woodrow Wilson and the Progressive Era 1910–17* (1954).

not solely an American tradition: it is in a sense every plain man's reaction to foreign politics, so it is natural that Tom Paine's latter-day English disciples should urge that diplomatic independence of America would enable Britain to cut herself off from America's wars (interpreted to mean the cold war and a possible third world war) just as Paine in his time argued a similar case for American independence.

Of course not all the left in Britain feels this way. Transferring to it Professor Schlesinger's classification of the American left between the Utopians and the pragmatists, we may say that the pragmatists (much the larger section) tend rather to be admirers of America as 'the efficiently-producing society', not marred by the class stratification of England, and are inclined to regard central heating and a good supply of frozen orange juice as more reasonable objects of endeavour than the new Jerusalem—a substitution that endears neither them nor America to the Utopians. Similarly, to the modernist right, the brisk young businessman element in the Conservative Party, America represents not merely a diplomatic bastion against revolution but 'the successful capitalist society', the proof that the system can really work, producing goods and freedom, and bestowing power, rewards, and prestige according to ability and success rather than inherited privilege. Only the traditionalist right, clinging to a value-system still paternalist and patrician, reacts with an antipathy equal to that of the radical left to a society where standards are set by majority taste. The political values of *The Loved One* and *The Quiet American* may be at opposite ends of the spectrum, but the reactions to America that they enshrine are closely akin.

In this fashion, the diplomatic alignment between the two powers, itself complex enough, is overlaid and given a sharp emotional edge by another relationship so broad

that it is difficult to find an adequate name for it: one
might call it the intellectual exchange. It is an outcome
of the accessibility of life and thought in each of the two
countries to the inspection of the other, and this of course
is chiefly a matter of language, though the relative familiarity of institutions such as the law and the political
system is also important. The sense of *terra incognita* with
which most people approach lives lived in other languages
than their own, and which usefully restrains judgement
and comparison, does not operate between English-
speaking countries. They suffer from what might be called
'instant comparability'. America is, and historically has
long been for many Englishmen, 'the alternative society',
the measuring-rod for their own way of life in a way no
other country could be. For each sector of political opinion
it may represent either what could be constructed or what
is being constructed at home, either shining example or
awful warning. And one obsessively discovers in the other
country evidence about what one hopes or fears for one's
own. The highly developed American and British literatures
of national introspection are very important to this process. Feiffer's subtly wounding blows at President Kennedy, Wright Mills's nightmares of the power élite, the
popular notion of the 'warfare state' sustained only by its
arms budgets, Professor Galbraith's elegant demonstration of the seamy side of affluence—all these strands of
American self-examination, enormously valuable and in-
structive when digested against a knowledge of the country
itself, make rather heady wine for foreigners when taken
without this balancer. The CND-supporting student, far
better versed than the average American in how many
ex-admirals are on the board of General Dynamics, is one
typical product of this intellectual cross-fertilization, though
there are more reassuring ones.

For Americans the alliance with Britain has lost in the

post-war period the emotional charge that it had earlier in this century, because the disparate sectors of political opinion usually lumped together in Europe as 'isolationists' have for various reasons assumed new foreign-policy stances. The particular kind of alliance with Britain which was at issue in the period before the first and second world wars was in some ways the hardest of all alliances for America to make. That is to say, the elements in American society which most resisted American involvement in Europe's affairs were resisting, as much as anything, the identification of Britain's enemies as America's: Irish Americans with inherited hostilities, German Americans unwilling to see their country at war with their fathers' country, those whose ethnic ties were with Scandinavia or Eastern Europe, tending to see Britain's ally, Russia, as hereditary enemy or Germany as hereditary friend. The reason why isolationism was strong in the Middle West was not, as Europeans assumed, because this part of the country was geographically remote from the outside world, but because these ethnic groups were strongly represented there. There were other kinds of American isolationism than that based on ethnic origin, but these also tended to be isolationist 'against' Britain. The left-idealist sector, somewhat akin to the radical element in the British Labour Party, and assuming American innocence of the wickedness of power politics, tended to identify the forces making for American war participation with international imperialist interests, whose home base was inevitably Britain. On the other hand, the right-nationalist isolationism, strong even now in the rank and file of the Republican Party, which has tended to prefer a go-it-alone position and xenophobically to spurn allies as mere burdens, tended also to be especially suspicious of Britain as a pre-eminently Machiavellian 'free-loader' on American effort. So one may say that all three main varieties of American isolationism—ethnic, left idealist, and right nationalist—contained a large element of distrust of Britain, and that therefore a straight alliance with Britain would probably have been the most likely of all arrangements to raise what remained of isolationist hackles, even in the post-war period.

However, precisely those sectors of U.S. opinion which were most prone to isolationism were also (with one exception) prone to an ardent anti-Communism. Irish-Catholic Americans reacting to the persecutor of the Church, German Americans reacting to the power that divided the fatherland and occupied half of it, East Europeans reacting to the oppressor of their relatives in the old country—for all these the anti-Communist alliance was the easiest of all alliances to accept. Only the left-idealist sector of the old isolationist cohorts remained unreconciled, and survives, much diminished, in the American peace movement, though no longer with an anti-British bias, since Britain is ambiguously blessed with the strongest of such post-war movements. All that remained in general American policy of the once-formidable tradition of isolationism after 1949 was the sense that the new policy was a regrettable though a necessary deviation from a happier past. Robert Sherwood in pre-Pearl Harbour days called the Anglo-American relationship a 'common-law alliance', less in the sense of one between countries adhering to the English common law, than on the analogy of 'common-law marriage', a *de facto* arrangement with a touch of sin about it, a hint of America's being seduced from her proper diplomatic celibacy to a mildly unfortunate entanglement. That tradition is not dead. And even now the choice of involvement to America's present degree in world politics is not automatically continued from administration to administration. It has to some extent to be renewed by every President. Since 1947 it has never appeared likely, assuming a prudent regard to the national interest, that any American President could conceive the world balance to be of such a nature that he had the option of reducing America's commitment to it. But the possibility of such a balance appearing to emerge within the foreseeable future cannot, in 1964, be dismissed.

The transformation in Britain's relation to the central power-balance, comparing the inter-war and the post-war years, was in some respects more profound and radical, and perhaps harder to take than the equivalent process for America. One can cast Britain as the Hamlet of the inter-war tragedy, her hesitations and ambivalences, her tendency to 'think too precisely on the event' as the main-spring of the drama. But for the post-war period the country has been obliged to say, in the words, appropriately enough, of that most notable exemplar of the intellectual exchange, Mr T. S. Eliot,

> . . . am not Prince Hamlet, nor was meant to be;
> Am an attendant lord: one that will do
> To swell a progress, start a scene or two.

To be demoted from protagonist to 'attendant lord', (or at best to 'Horatio, his friend'), that is to find that the central decisions must be taken elsewhere, and that the cultivation of influence must replace the exercise of power would have been a hard enough adjustment to make in the best of circumstances, quite aside from the other adjustments that Britain has had to make. But it was an inescapable one, since the war had destroyed the old European balance, and had left only the possibility of a world balance, in which the main Western weight would inevitably be America. In the event it was taken with surprising speed and lack of hesitation. The year 1939 was the last year of decay of the old balance: less than ten years later the new one was almost articulated.

The revival of the alliance

The most reasonable date to asssign to the revival of the Anglo-American alliance, or the beginning of its post-war phase, is 1948, since that year saw the coming into operation of the joint diplomatic-military enterprise of creating a balance of power against Russia in Europe. The obvious sign of this joint enterprise was the setting in train of the negotiations that led in April 1949 to the signature of the North Atlantic treaty. But there was an equal significance in the British decision, taken almost casually in July 1948, to accept the stationing in East Anglia of the B-29 bombers, the means of delivery of the atomic bombs which at that time were the only substantial American sanction against a Russian advance westward. One may call this the beginning of the 'Airstrip One' relationship of Britain to America. The general construction of the Western balance against Russia spreads, of course, over a longer period, from early 1947 when America first accepted the necessity of involvement in the central power-balance in peacetime, to mid-1949 when the actual mechanism of NATO was completed and formally ratified. By the end of 1949 the original cold-war order of battle, east and west, was fairly complete, even to the establishment of Yugoslavia's equivocal situation. But 1948 is the year in which the Anglo-American relationship assumed its characteristic shape in this phase of the post-war conflict, that of Britain as the most committed (though not the most docile) of America's lieutenants in the business of resisting the encroachment of Russian power. Even, perhaps, a lieutenant who had conceived the basic idea of the enterprise, for there is no doubt that Bevin was as active an originator of the Western alliance structure as Acheson, and that Churchill was its most powerful public advocate. (Lester Pearson was almost equally a 'founding father'.

The treaty is expressly tailored to fulfil the central condition for an effective and domestically palatable Canadian foreign policy: that it should keep British and American policies in line in the North Atlantic area.) It was Bevin's note to Washington of February 1947 on Greece and Turkey which induced the formulation of the Truman Doctrine, and in a much more genuine sense than Canning had done in 1823, called the New World in to redress the balance of power of the Old. His role was also decisive in seizing on the idea presented—at first fairly vaguely— in the original speech by General Marshall in June 1947, which became the basis of the Marshall plan. Bevin's was the enthusiasm, the drive, and the determination which shepherded the European powers in the direction he thought they and the Americans should go. His was the device of the Brussels Pact, of early 1948, which laid the ground plan for the military organization of NATO. And in all this he was very conscious that for Britain the relationship with America was the heart of the matter, however much the result might need to be disguised as an equalitarian multilateral treaty organization of the North Atlantic powers.

But realistically one must concede that America in 1948–9 regarded herself primarily as entering an anti-Communist coalition, which included Britain among other powers, rather than a general-purpose alliance with Britain. And many members of Bevin's own party were prepared to accept the new arrangements only as a necessary mode of restraining immediate Stalinist ambitions in Europe, until something better could be arranged, rather than as a general alignment with America. One cannot discount the significance of the left and liberal opinion of the immediate post-war period, which had seen Britain's future as a bridge or third force between Russia and America, rather than as a predestined ally of America.

Nor should one ignore other real clashes of policy and interest between the two countries at the time. Each was greatly exasperated with the other over Palestine, many Americans were strongly suspicious of the Labour government as socialistic or even communistic, and the British were disappointed and irritated over the conditions of the U.S. loan, and the end of lend-lease. Given these frictions, and the generally fairly radical temper of opinion of the 1945 Parliamentary Labour Party (if not of Attlee's government) it might seem a plausible argument that, had Stalin's policy in 1945-6 been less intransigent, or less conditioned by Marxist assumptions about the capitalist world, the post-war realignment would have been somewhat like that after the first world war, with a considerable estrangement between Britain and America.

But any view of the Anglo-American alliance as an almost accidental by-product of Stalinist foreign policy has to be set against the historical attitude of Britain to America's place in the world balance. From Valley Forge or Yorktown to the present day one can say that the essential British relation to America has been that of progressive adaptation to the growth in American power. First, from the thirteen rebellious colonies to (by 1823) a power of some substance, already in the Monroe Doctrine claiming a sort of hegemony in her own hemisphere. Then, between 1823 and 1898, to the consolidation of that power, and her evolution into one of the great powers. Then in the twentieth century from one of a half-dozen great powers to one of the two dominant powers. At every stage in this growth there have been frictions and conflicts of interest between Britain and America. For much of the nineteenth century a third war between them seemed probable. But, equally, since 1823 there has been a sort of intuition or premonition in British foreign policy that America would in due course prove a decisive weight in the world balance, and one whose role would not, in the last analysis, be disadvantageous to Britain.

The obvious reason for dating this strand in British policy from 1823 is, of course, Canning's part in the events that led to the enunciation of the Monroe Doctrine. Even bearing in mind the conflicts between British and American policy, the British dislike of the possibility of an American empire based on the Caribbean, the American suspicion that Britain might be intending to line her own imperial pockets with some of the Spanish colonies, and their general rivalry in Latin America for the rest of the nineteenth century, one may still regard as significant the basic assumption of interests in common *vis-à-vis* the Continental powers that underlay the British policy of the time, if not the American. It was an assumption obviously at odds with the realities of the next eighty years. The 'manifest destiny to overspread the continent allotted by Providence' that was the dominant impulse of nineteenth-century American policy brought the U.S. more often into conflict with British than with any other European interests, on the general position of Canada, on the Panama Isthmus, on the Maine and Oregon boundaries, and on the Venezuela issue. Open rupture was just avoided at the Civil War period: some people in Britain were inclined to see the possible end of the Union chiefly as the end of a dangerous power rival of Britain. (This was so tenable a view in many ways that it is perhaps rather surprising that it never came to be a predominant one.) But through these frictions one may discern a tacit *arrière-pensée* that relations with America did not quite fall within the normal categories of power politics. Perhaps 1896 can be regarded as the date of a firm decision by Britain that the normal sort of power competition between sovereign states must not be the mode of her relationship with the U.S. The surprising mildness of reaction in Westminster

B

to the markedly jingoistic handling by Cleveland of the crisis over Venezuela would seem to indicate as much. One must be apologetically conscious of the benefit in this process of a sort of racialism, or at any rate an Anglo-Saxon self-consciousness of the Kipling–Rhodes variety that produces contemporary discomfort, expressed at its most fervent in Joseph Chamberlain's well-known reflection of May 1898: 'terrible as war may be, even war itself would be cheaply purchased if, in a great and noble cause, the Stars and Stripes and the Union Jack should wave together over an Anglo-Saxon alliance'. The British consciousness of isolation from all the European powers over the Boer War, the American consciousness that all the European powers save Britain were on the Spanish side during the Spanish-American war, undoubtedly reinforced the sense of a common power interest. The settlement of the Isthmus issue in 1901, taken together with the Venezuela settlement and the British attitude in the Spanish-American war, may be regarded as ending the original British ambivalence to the Monroe Doctrine and conceding the American claim (by now, with Teddy Roosevelt, quite explicit) to hegemony in the Western hemisphere. The Alaska settlement was similarly evidence of the fact that the cultivation of easy relations with the U.S. was now a primary British interest in that hemisphere, one to which even some Canadian interests might be sacrificed. And the sense of a joint power interest in Anglo-American control of the Atlantic, a joint interest critically threatened by German submarine successes, must be conceded as a major element in American involvement in 1917. The Senate's repudiation of Versailles, the failure of Wilson's policy, and the Republican landslide of the 1920 election mark the one really substantial and complete reversal in almost a century's growing tendency on America's part to seek her full share in the management of the world. The

revulsion towards pacifism and opting out of the balance
that dominated U.S. opinion in the 1920s and 1930s was a
perhaps inevitable reaction to the first real American
understanding of the costs involved in such a role. Yet
even in the 1920s one can see at least in the Pacific the
growth of U.S. involvement, and its concomitants for
British policy in the Anglo-American *entente*, the abandonment of British efforts to compete with the U.S. in the
field of naval power, and the sacrifice of the Anglo-
Japanese alliance.

To take this view is not necessarily to claim any great
prescience or Machiavellianism for the makers of British
foreign policy: the policy line can as well be attributed to
prejudice and instinct as to calculation. Two episodes in
the 1930s are sometimes cited as evidence that when the
American government in fact showed itself willing to play
an active part in maintaining the world balance, it was
thwarted on each occasion by British faintheartedness.
The first of these episodes was the Stimson note of 1932 on
Manchuria. The second that of January 1938, when
Chamberlain threw cold water on Roosevelt's tentative
bid towards a world conference, because he feared that it
might prove a pointless diversion from his own policy in
Europe. But if Stimson was willing to involve American
strength in resistance to Japan the President, Hoover, was
not, and the dispassionate American historians of the 1938
episode, Langer and Gleason,[2] are more sceptical than
Eden as to Roosevelt's intentions.

So that it is not altogether unreasonable to interpret the
process by which the 'unavowed alliance'—the Anglo-
American alliance before 1949—originally came into being
as that of the conscious or unconscious resignation by
Britain to America of her own place in the order of world
power—first her ambitions in the American hemisphere

[2] *The Challenge to Isolation, 1937–40* (1952).

(by 1901), then her hopes of an independent course in the Pacific (with the Japanese alliance as its basis), then the two-power naval standard, or naval superiority or equality of any sort. In line with this theory one may point out that the rise of America to world power—so potentially threatening to the values and power of the Old World— was never met by the traditional European answer to such development, a balance-of-power coalition, and that this was because 'meta-political' factors in the relationship of Britain and America ensured that Britain, the traditional and in the naval sense essential leader of such a coalition, did not seriously consider organizing anything of the sort, intuitively assuming that American and British interests would in the end prove complementary in the central con- flicts of international politics.

Given that the American stance since 1947 in Europe might be regarded as a sort of culmination of this process, a final adoption of the traditional British policy of the balance-of-power coalition, ought one to regard the formal mechanism of that coalition, the NATO alliance, as a preferable or as a *faute de mieux* form of the Anglo-American alliance? And if the formation of NATO had *not* proved possible at that time, would a straight bilateral alliance, or an alliance between Britain, Canada, and America have proved so? The evolution of American opinion between 1946 and 1949 was so rapid and radical that there were only thirteen dissentients in the Senate, when the North Atlantic treaty was ratified, to the twenty-year involve- ment of America in Europe's affairs, a step that would have seemed unthinkable to most Americans three years earlier. Moreover, the only condition likely to have pre- vented NATO in its present form emerging in 1949 would have been that the left in France and Italy had proved strong enough to prevent it, and such a development would have alarmed U.S. opinion into any available alliance. But in any case NATO was in several respects an even more convenient alliance for Britain than a direct bilateral treaty with America would have been, for it combined the long-sought diplomatic alignment with America with a renewal of ties to her traditional allies in Europe and a rationalization of the position of Canada. Strategically speaking, it not only established an Anglo-American frontier, but put it as far east as possible, on the Elbe rather than the Channel. The only condition which would have made NATO a less desirable arrangement for Britain than a bilateral treaty would have been if it had reduced British influence in Washington to match that of other NATO members.

On the historical evidence of 1949–63, one may say that this clearly did not happen. Whether or not de Gaulle's ascription of an Anglo-American directorate to NATO represents an exaggeration of the degree of British influence, one can hardly deny that though NATO maintains the sovereign equality of its members, some have been visibly more equal than others. As far as the minor members of NATO are concerned, this is no more than the continuance in its counsels of the normal and conventional distinction between great powers and small. And one could add that special historical factors have conditioned the situation of Germany, and that Italy is 'marginal' between the major and the minor members, again continuing her traditional position among the powers. As to France, up to 1958 an element of historical hang-over from 1940, and the instability of the Fourth Republic, were major influences. The lingering remnants of the special personal relations of the war also had some influence. The U.S. experience of alliance in 1941–5 was substantially the experience of alliance with Britain: the minor powers and the exiled governments were dependants rather than allies, and with Russia the relation was always so wary, friction-ridden, and ambivalent that it might be regarded as co-belligerency rather than alliance.

These factors account in part for the particular quality of Anglo-American relations within NATO. But even giving them due weight it is hardly possible to ignore the importance of an Anglo-American strategic connexion which was anterior to the formal alliance of NATO, continued alongside it but not under its control, and represented at least until 1957 a more decisive element of the total Western military sanction against Russia than NATO forces did. This was the connexion in advanced weapons. (It is difficult to use any more specific term: first atomic bombs, then nuclear ones, then missile systems have been the crucial elements.) The reason why 1948 must be regarded as the formative year of the Anglo-American alliance was not only the setting under way of the joint enterprise of NATO, but the decision to station Strategic Air Command (SAC) bombers, then the major component of U.S. military power, in East Anglia. (It may be emphasized, since the point is often overlooked, that both American and British long-range strike aircraft have until recently been independent of and outside NATO control.)

The advanced-weapons relationship

Arguably, this advanced-weapons relationship, the central Anglo-American strategic relationship, has been the chief factor determining general diplomatic choices for Britain since 1948. Like other aspects of Anglo-American relations it has included elements of conflict and ambivalence. The whole history of the independent British deterrent can be seen in fact as a memorial to the uncertainties within it. The strategic co-operation side of the relationship, represented by the stationing of U.S. bombers in East Anglia, was agreed in the context of a particularly

tense moment of the blockade of Berlin, at a time when
the CIA allegedly were unwilling to predict the continuance of peace for more than sixty days ahead, when
General Clay believed that war was imminent, and when
SAC bases in Britain would have been a higher priority
target for a Russian strike than either the Polaris or the
Thor bases later, since they then represented a far more
substantial part of total American military power, in fact
almost the whole of it. Forrestal indicates the degree of his
surprise at the casual and unquestioning nature of the
British acceptance;[3] Attlee hardly discusses the question.[4]
This was of course well before the change in the nature of
warfare was fully understood, even in political circles.
The second, or 'reinsurance' element of the advanced-
weapons relationship, the British initiative to create an
independent strength in this field, had developed even
earlier in the pre-NATO period. From 1942, when co-
operation between Britain and America on the atomic
bomb programme had first become formal, it was consistently accompanied by frictions which were kept to a
comparatively subdued level during the war only by the
personal diplomacy of Churchill. The understandings he
reached with Roosevelt did not percolate far down the
American chain of command: in fact they were solidly
blocked by General Groves, as the General pointed out
himself with a certain pride during the Oppenheimer
hearing. '. . . I was not responsible for our close cooperation with the British. I did everything to hold back on it.
. . . I did not carry out the wishes of our Government with
respect to cooperation with the British because I was lean-
ing over backwards.'[5] A few days after the Japanese sur-

---

[3] *The Forrestal Diaries*, ed. Walter Millis (1951).
[4] See Francis Williams, *A Prime Minister Remembers* (1961) and C. R.
Attlee, *As It Happened* (1954).
[5] U.S. Atomic Energy Commission, *In the Matter of J. Robert Oppenheimer;
transcript of hearing before Personnel Security Board, 1954*, p. 175.

render, in August 1945, Senator McMahon introduced the Bill which a year later became the Act usually known by his name, which effectively cut off Britain, along with America's other allies, from access to American work in the atomic field. Some degree of guilt-feeling about the justice of the McMahon Act as regards Britain was felt almost immediately in the American administration, since, as Admiral Strauss admits, the two wartime agreements— the Quebec agreement of August 1943 and the Hyde Park agreement of September 1944—had been 'solemn undertakings'[6] between Roosevelt and Churchill, intended to bind successor governments. The Hyde Park agreement provided for full collaboration between the American and British governments in developing fissionable material for military and commercial purposes after the war, unless there was a termination by joint agreement. 'It had, of course, been effectively breached by the McMahon Act, whose congressional draftsmen were unaware of the existence of such a contract. This must also have been the situation of President Truman when he signed the bill into law.'[7] (This statement is a little difficult to reconcile with the evidence, for even though the American copy of the Hyde Park agreement was officially lost for the entire period of the Truman administration, from 1944 to 1953, it is impossible to believe that the British expostulators did not flourish their own copy.) The breakdown of co-operation between Britain and America is usually attributed to the security scandals over Nunn May and Fuchs, but in fact it occurred some years before most of these troubles. Looking at the sentiments expressed by Senators and others at the time, one is inclined to feel that it was a matter of general nationalist feeling, plus the intricacies of the struggle between the military and others for control of

---

[6] L. L. Strauss, *Men and Decisions* (1962), pp. 369–74.
[7] Ibid., p. 370.

the atomic field in America, competitive instincts over the supposed commercial prospects (whose immediate potential was greatly exaggerated), the continuing personal influences of General Groves and others, and the complication presented by the plans for international control of atomic energy. The British naturally tended to emphasize their contribution to the development of the bomb, and the rights it conferred, while the Americans tended to feel that whatever might be the case in this respect, the British should relinquish any privileges they had exacted from Roosevelt, in consideration of general American benefits received.[8] Senator McMahon apparently had no knowledge of the agreements until Churchill told him about them in a visit to Washington in January 1952, but Attlee seems to have assumed that such knowledge would not in any case have affected the outcome since 'The Senate wanted everything for America'.[9]

When the direction of American policy became clear in Britain, Attlee did make an effort to modify it: he and Sir John Anderson, then Chairman of the U.K. Advisory Committee on Atomic Energy, visited Washington in November 1945, for talks with Truman and Byrnes, but any understandings reached broke down almost at once. By January 1946 the resolution on an independent British programme (which inevitably held in itself the prospect of weapons as well as power) seems to have been firm: the construction of the Harwell establishment began three months later. The decision to proceed with the actual making of weapons was first made public in May 1948: it had been reached in the Defence Committee and announced to the Cabinet some weeks earlier.[10] The programme

---

[8] See, for example, Senator Vandenberg's view in *The Private Papers of Senator Vandenberg* (1952).

[9] *A Prime Minister Remembers*, pp. 95–118.

[10] See correspondence between R. H. S. Crossman and G. K. Strauss, *Encounter*, June-Aug. 1963.

called for the testing of a British atomic device by 1952, a date duly kept, though the first 'droppable bomb' was not produced until a year later. When Attlee's government began this programme, the Russians had not yet built an atomic weapon and were not expected to do so until 1952, so that Britain may have expected to be a sort of 'equal second' with Russia in the field, but the Russians, driven by a more urgent incentive, outpaced the Western expectations of their performance, and tested their first bomb three years sooner, in August 1949.

In this early period, the decisions on construction of atomic weapons were seen by the statesmen concerned as no different in kind from those on other aspects of the defence establishment. Attlee has outlined the reasons as he saw them for Britain:

Once Congress proceeded to pass the McMahon Bill we had to go ahead on our own. . . . At that time we had to bear in mind that there was always the possibility of their [the Americans] withdrawing and becoming isolationist once again. The manufacture of a British atom bomb was therefore at that stage essential to our defence. You must remember that all this was prior to NATO. NATO has altered things. But at that time although we were doing our best to make the Americans see the realities of the European situation—the world situation —we couldn't be sure we'd succeed. . . . Meanwhile we had to face the world as it was. We had to look to our defence. . . .[11]

No doubt the decision might have been reconsidered in 1949, when NATO was established, or in 1950, after the attack in Korea, when the first serious effort to rebuild the conventional strength of the NATO powers in Europe was undertaken, and understanding increased of the difficulties inherent in military reliance on atomic wepons. But for good or ill the progress of British technology in this field, which was by 1958 to produce a modification of

[11] *A Prime Minister Remembers*, pp. 118–19.

the McMahon Act sharply favourable to Britain as against other U.S. allies, had already begun to pay off in some degree of advantage by 1948. The first easing of the American position in Britain's favour was the *modus vivendi* known as the Blair House agreement of January 1948, which established nine areas of research (none having any relation to weapons) in which information might be exchanged. This seems to have been in part a *quid pro quo* for the waiver, on the British side, of the British right of veto on American use of atomic weapons which had been embodied in the Quebec agreement. At least this is the impression given by Forrestal's and Vandenberg's accounts, and when Churchill published the text of the Quebec agreement in the spring of 1954 it was apparently (if Lord Cherwell's understanding was accurate) with the notion that the Labour attack on British inability to influence American policy on tests ought to be turned against those who had waived British rights in 1948.[12] If the Labour government did make this exchange, it would not be surprising, since progress in the economic uses of nuclear energy was a major element in the visions of a future world of plenty that cheered these peculiarly bleak years of post-war reconstruction, and the veto right must have seemed likely to remain ineffective anyway, in view of the general American attitude to the Quebec agreement.

Nor was late 1950–early 1951, despite the renewed emphasis on conventional forces, a likely time for the Labour government to make a decision that America should become sole guardian of atomic weapons for the West. In fact this period, the period of the approach to the Yalu River in Korea and the involvement of the United Nations in hostilities with China, was the moment of sharpest alienation from America of left-wing opinion in Britain during the entire post-war period. A few

[12] See Cherwell's letter, in Strauss, p. 371.

months later, at the end of 1951, Churchill's government inherited the atomic-weapons programme which by then was within hail of actually producing an atomic device. The first test was held a year after the Conservative accession to office. The new Prime Minister had not yet developed his later concern with the dangers of nuclear war, and though one of his main preoccupations was the reduction of the arms budget, this dictated retention, not abandonment, of the atomic-weapons programme, since it was the post-Korea rebuilding of conventional forces which constituted the main burden on manpower and other resources.

Churchill in fact made a determined personal bid, especially after the inauguration of President Eisenhower, to restore the situation of Britain *vis-à-vis* American research to something approaching what it had been in 1945, when he left office. In this his chief asset was the independent British acquirement of technological skills in the atomic field. As Lewis Strauss, the major American policy maker saw it, 'the information the British already possessed could not be erased from their knowledge, and they were making further advances and discoveries', and he therefore recommended that the area of information exchanged should be enlarged to include 'the effects on human beings and their environment of the blast, heat and radiation resulting from atomic explosions'.[13] At this time, in November 1952, the Americans had had their first success with thermonuclear weapons, and the Russians were to reach the same stage nine months later, in August 1953. Some knowledge of the extra dimension of destruction that had been brought to warfare began to be available to Churchill in late 1953—early 1954, and began notably to affect his attitudes to relations between Russia and the West, and through his remarkable speeches also

[13] Ibid., p. 372.

profoundly to affect other people's attitudes, especially in Britain. But his initial reaction to disclosures of the power of thermonuclear weapons was the belief that, compared to atomic weapons, they somewhat evened the odds between the two dominant powers and the rest of the world, since even the dominant powers were now vulnerable, whereas the degree of danger to the small powers, such as Britain, could not be increased since it was already total. Thus as far as Britain was concerned, the case for maintaining her autonomous co-operative stance *vis-à-vis* America seemed no less pressing than it had been in 1946. The technological distance between an atomic device and a thermonuclear bomb is much shorter than the distance between starting-point and an atomic device, so that the decision that Britain should move from the manufacture of fission to fusion weapons followed without much questioning.

The conventional-strategy relationship: Europe

However, before we consider the next stage of the advanced-weapons relationship, we must look at the other side of the strategic context, that of conventional weapons. That is to say we must look at the growth of NATO, and of the European movement.[14]

From the earliest post-war years there were two rival impulses at work in the making of Europe. One might call them the Atlantic and the Carolingian impulse— Atlantic for obvious reasons, Carolingian rather more for the present *grand Charles* than for the original one. The Atlantic impulse hardly needs definition: it is the one that

[14] The author is apologetically conscious that she is repeating in what follows about Europe the substance of her earlier article, 'The Diplomatic Meanings of Europe' published in C. Bell, ed., *Europe Without Britain* (1963). But it is impossible to give an account of two sides of this triangle without saying a good deal about the third.

sees Western Europe as the natural ally and protégé of America, the eastern wing of the Atlantic Community. The Carolingian view is centered on the Rhine rather than the Atlantic: it sees Western Europe (or in more ambitious versions Europe *tout court*) as a notable and nuclear-armed power, controlling its own destinies, certainly no longer a protégé of America and perhaps not *inevitably* an ally. In balance-of-power terms the Atlantic concept of Europe's future implies a continuance of the essentially bilateral balance that has existed for most of the post-war period; the Carolingian concept implies that this bilateral balance is being or may be transformed into a multilateral balance of the traditional sort.

It is not at all accurate to date the emergence of the Carolingian view only from the time of de Gaulle's re-accession to power in 1958, for its possibility has been implicit in the European movement for the whole of the post-war period, even though up to 1956 it hardly amounted to more than an anti-American gleam in various European eyes. In fact, the whole process of 'making Europe' has depended on an interaction of the two impulses, with the Atlantic one dominant only in the early period. The original parentage was certainly Atlantic, France and America rather than France and Germany. To say this is not to deny the conventional view that the initiative that produced 'Europe of the Six' represented a French diplomatic effort to solve the problem that had haunted France since 1870, the problem of German power. It is only to point out that the French decisions of 1950 which produced the ECSC and the EDC were dependent on the earlier French decision of 1947, the decision to accept Marshall aid and therewith the tacit status of an American ally. This was a temporarily decisive turning-point, but until it was taken in 1947 France had pretty much the look of a country whose natural position in the developing conflict between America and Russia would be ambivalent. The domestic political situation, with the Communists as the largest single party and the engrossers of 25 per cent of the vote was one pointer in this direction, and so, rather more, were France's diplomatic interests as traditionally interpreted. For France was confronted after the second world war, as after the first, with one overwhelming diplomatic problem: the certainty that Germany would rise again, and that her Anglo-Saxon allies were not likely to endorse the projects (fragmentation, separation of the Rhineland) which were suggested to offset this danger on both occasions. But there was one decisive difference between 1919 and 1946, as far as the counterbalancing of Germany was concerned. Whereas in 1919 Russia had been seen as an enigma out of which no good for the capitalist world was likely to come, in 1945 she seemed a logical, promising and powerful ally, and moreover, not as a counterbalance against Germany only, but against 'the Anglo-Saxons', as de Gaulle himself had mused earlier: 'At the same time her [Russia's] presence in the Allied camp brought France a balancing element against the Anglo-Saxons, of which I was determined to make use.'[15]

It is not surprising that despite these preoccupations France nevertheless found it necessary when the crisis came, in May 1947, to drop any ambitions for balancing between Russia and 'the Anglo-Saxons', and to line up with America's other protégés in Western Europe. No French government other than one actually dominated by the Communist Party could have refused American economic aid in that 1947 situation. And of course 'the American alliance' is an even older preoccupation of French diplomacy than 'the Russian alliance', dating back to the French treaty of 1778 with Britain's thirteen

[15] *The Call to Honour* (N.Y., 1955), p. 225.

rebellious colonies. One might also say that the formalization of the American alliance with Europe in 1949, in the North Atlantic treaty, was a late fulfilment of Clemenceau's demand thirty years earlier, in 1919, for a cast-iron American guarantee of French security.

However, the point being made here is that the relationship accepted with America in 1947, and the necessity of putting France's other diplomatic commitments into a framework in which this was the dominant element, conditioned the whole of the early French endeavour to 'faire l'Europe', from 1950. The French policies which produced the ECSC and EDC were essentially prompted by the need to reconcile French interests with the unfolding pattern of American policy, that is of finding a *modus vivendi* with the other embryonic American ally, West Germany, still occupied and diplomatically passive as she then was. The prospect of German industrial revival, in particular the level of German production of coal and steel, was the issue on which the problem of reconciling French to American policy first became acute. France by the beginning of 1950 had to face the imminent rebirth of a Germany which would clearly within the foreseeable future not only be sovereign but possessed of a substantial arms capacity. It was this situation that produced the Schuman Plan, which eventually evolved into the European Coal and Steel Community. In essence this turn in French policy was away from the effort to adjust her power-position *vis-à-vis* Germany through the traditional diplomatic devices of the national state, and towards a new effort to make the adjustment by modifying the framework of the national state. The problem was an old one: the solution new. If we ask why, at this point, the French began to seek so radical a means of coping with so familiar a problem, we must look to the other, the Carolingian impulse in policy.

The notion of some merging of sovereignties in Europe is, of course, an old one. It can as well be represented as a return to a former pattern—the united Christendom of Western Europe, out of which the sharp sovereignties of the modern world emerged—as the evolution of something new. (The combination of appeals that this makes possible —'Back to the Golden Age' as well as 'Forward to the Golden Age'—has been a great source of strength to the movement, reconciling the temperaments of the conservative and the radical.) What was new in 1950 was not the idea of European integration but a political constellation that favoured its fortunes. At the top policy-making level this constellation was simply the three leaders chiefly concerned: Schuman in France, Adenauer in Germany, and De Gasperi in Italy. It must be regarded as one of those coincidences that amount to historical events that these three statesmen were not only of similar religious and political complexions—all Catholics and all Christian Democrats—but that they should all three epitomize in their personal histories the meeting-points of Latin and Teutonic civilization in Europe. Few European leaders could have had better reasons for personal scepticism about the sacrosanctity of national sovereignty or of the frontier lines that Europe happened to be endowed with for the time being. And aside from these leaders there was, of course, the intellectual movement, not at the level of the man in the street, but at the level of officials or potential officials and 'opinion leaders' like parliamentarians and journalists, which was sceptical about, or disgusted with, the national state as such. Those who had lived through and reflected on the Europe of the 1930s and 1940s could hardly have failed to be strongly conscious of the inadequacy of the national state—inadequacy to protect the individual in war or to assure his economic well-being in peace—and more than its inadequacy, its poten-

c

tiality for evil, as demonstrated in the rise of Hitler. It was hardly surprising that some of them should seek to promote an alternative loyalty.

The chief reason for the difference in British and Continental attitudes in the crucial period 1948–55 was that this factor of disillusionment with the performance of the national state—their own national state—hardly existed in Britain. After all, the experiences respectively of Britain and the Continent during the war had been wholly different. Where the Continental Europeans felt forcibly in their own lives the defeat and the breakdown of their political communities, the British experience was of the unexpected solidity and endurance of their particular political community under a heavy battering, and *its ability to survive despite the loss of all Britain's traditional allies in Western Europe, and the unification of the Continent against her*. With the help of her overseas connexions, in America and the Commonwealth, Britain was able not only to survive this situation but to become one of the architects of the final victory and one of the makers of the post-war world. If the diplomatic lesson of the war to Continental Europe seemed to be the inadequacy of the national state, for Britain it seemed to be that her survival depended less on her traditional Continental allies than on her overseas connexions, especially the 'unavowed alliance' with America. It is thus not surprising that in the post-war period Britain was far less oriented to supra-national experiments in European integration than the Continental powers, and that above all she should have been resolute against any but the Atlantic impulse as far as European union was concerned. The basic determination behind British foreign policy in the early post-war years was not to be committed in Europe more than an inch or two deeper than America would venture.

The Brussels treaty is no contradiction of this. Bevin

always regarded it, in the words of one of his closest
lieutenants, as 'a sprat to catch a whale'. The 'whale' in
its final form, of course, was NATO—the perfect instrumentality, from the British point of view, for reconciling
her strategic interests on the Continent with the necessity
of maintaining a close alignment with the overseas connexions whose strength made effective British intervention there possible. The 'overseas connexions' in this case
meant not just the United States but also Canada directly,
and later Australia and New Zealand indirectly, though
the actual instrumentality in the second case, the ANZUS
treaty, was in itself rather distasteful to Britain. That does
not alter the fact that these treaties represented for Britain,
in the alignment that they ensured with America, not only
a solution to her own security problems, but a solution to
the security problems of the older members of the Commonwealth, to whom she had still real defensive and political
and emotional commitments.

The Atlantic impulse being satisfactorily embodied in
an institutional form with NATO, Britain felt no real
urge to show much more than a token interest in schemes
of strictly European integration. The history of the Council of Europe is a monument to this fact. And the British
disinclination to be any more deeply committed than the
U.S. in Europe is reflected in the original British refusal
to commit troops to the European army under the EDC
treaty. Once the EDC treaty had actually been destroyed
by the French Assembly, of course, Britain had to revise
her position and commit four divisions to the EDC's non-
supranational successor and substitute, the Western European Union. This was no late-arising Carolingian movement of opinion: it was a conscious sacrifice of a preferred
position in order to save an even more valued element in
policy, the Atlantic orientation of Europe. The angry
reaction in America to the end of the EDC and Dulles's

earlier mutterings about an 'agonizing reappraisal' of
America's alliance structure in Europe threatened an
achievement more valued in Downing Street than in the
Élysée.

It is tempting to ascribe the failure of the EDC to its
being neither satisfactorily Atlantic nor satisfactorily
Carolingian, inadequate in the first because it was confined to the Continental powers, inadequate in the second
because it had come to seem too obviously an instrument
of American foreign policy. But many other factors went
to its rejection. Armed forces are, after all, the centre of a
state's sovereignty, or the means whereby that sovereignty
is asserted, and it is not surprising that a state should balk
at surrendering control over them even when it has
swallowed much else.

Relations outside Europe: Asia and the Pacific

The end of Acheson's period in office and the beginning
of that of Dulles in 1953 mark the onset of a period when
American relations with Europe deteriorated rather
steeply. This has often been put down simply to Dulles's
diplomatic hamhandedness. But though Dulles may often
have driven his European *vis-à-vis* to say of him, as was
said of Aberdeen, that he was a good man in the worst
sense of the term, the root cause of the deterioration of
relations in his period of office may be found in the fact
that whereas the crises of Acheson's time were chiefly in
Europe, except for Korea, those during Dulles's conduct
of affairs, 1953–8, were mostly outside Europe—Indo-
China, Formosa, Quemoy and Matsu, Suez, Syria and
Lebanon, and the whole post-Bandung business of relations with neutrals. The second round of the Berlin crisis
did not begin until a time, November 1958, when illness
had almost wrested the direction of policy from Dulles's

grasp, and in his one great crisis of Western relations with Russia in Europe, 1956, he clearly decided almost from the first to do nothing.

In general one may say that whereas issues affecting the balance of power in Europe have been the *casus foederis*, the occasion of alliance, for Britain and America, issues arising outside Europe—in Latin America, in Canada, in the Pacific, and above all in the Middle East—have on the whole been occasions of friction and dissension between them. In the world outside Europe, each is tolerant and large-minded where the other's interests are concerned. The British take the larger view regarding Vietnam or Cuba, the Americans regarding Suez or Katanga. Few intellectual attitudes come more naturally in any country than a large-minded tolerance towards damage to the interests of an ally. Even now, the alliance that is sturdy enough in the central balance is rather fragile in the peripheral areas. Britain is excluded from ANZUS still, and is a rather unenthusiastic ally in SEATO: America is not formally in CENTO. The greatest single cause of difference in foreign policies in the post-war period has been their respective attitudes to China, the greatest single crisis in relations that over Suez, the sharpest recent frictions those over the Congo.

The conflicts in the world outside Europe have been conflicts of interest in part, but also conflicts of historic outlook, with Britain espousing diplomatic principles that are traditional and perhaps cynical, but in general oriented to compromise and balancing, tacitly assuming that one can rub along even with an enemy if one does not allow moral enthusiasm for his defeat to overcome one's judgement. The obvious example of this has been in East Asia, in the question of relations with the present government in Peking. The American historic relation to China has been marked by a genuine benevolence, if a

paternalist one, whereas Britain's relations with that
country were not, to put it mildly, one of the more credit-
able episodes in her nineteenth-century history. Yet since
1950 British policy has been much readier than American
to promote a tolerable *modus vivendi* between China and
the rest of the world. In part this mildness has been dictated by prudence. British power in East Asia after the
war was reaching towards the base point of sixty years of
steady decline. The causes of this decline were twofold: on
the one hand a growth in relative strength of those powers
against whom her own strength had to be measured, and
on the other an increase in commitments elsewhere which
reduced the margin available for use in the Pacific towards
the vanishing line. The Anglo-Japanese alliance of 1902
marks the first recognition by Britain that her power
could no longer readily be stretched as far as the Pacific,
which must always be a third or fourth priority theatre
when Britain is involved in a general security crisis. The
first priority must be the home islands and home waters
and the Atlantic, since if defeat is experienced there it
means the end of resistance; the second must be help to
what allies she can muster on the Continent; the third
must be (or at least has been in the past) the Middle East,
which has meant oil for the fleet, and the safeguarding of
the Indian base and communications with the rest of the
Commonwealth. The Pacific has characteristically had to
rub along with what can be spared from other areas. This
order of priorities was illustrated in the second world war,
in the necessary acceptance of acquiescence in the loss of
much of the then British Empire in South East Asia, and
the arguments over supplies for the Burma–China theatre
of war.

Events after the second world war further accentuated
the decline in British power in the Pacific. Conventional
naval forces, the traditional base of British strength there,

were devalued in two respects. They were quite irrelevant to the main military threat in the areas round China's periphery, the guerrilla in the jungles or the mountains, and almost as irrelevant *vis-à-vis* China herself, a power which does not compete in naval strength and whose main cities are inland. (Naval-based air power, as in the U.S. Seventh Fleet, is of course quite a different proposition.) The colonial transformation made the retention of even the Singapore base for more than a few years seem rather unlikely, and reduced responsibilities as well as strength. Finally, the increased commitment of troops in peace-time to Europe through NATO reduced general British ability to provide forces for emergencies elsewhere, for instance in Malaysia.

The place of the Pacific and Asia in the American scale of priorities has been very different from its place in the British scale, and this has accounted not only for past differences in attitudes to Japan, but also for the chief continuing divergence in post-war policy, that over China. America, unlike Britain, lives in the Pacific, and has to think of the East Asian states as a set of neighbours, the group of powers who share with her the shores of that ocean, and who must affect her security interests in quite a direct and immediate manner. This puts the area well up in the national scale of foreign-policy priorities for all Americans, and first in that scale for some. That most of the 'Asia firsters' in America have been Republicans is not merely a matter of the geographic division of party support: it is rather that the Democrats became identified in Woodrow Wilson's time as the party of intervention in Europe, and the Republicans seem, as it were, to have identified themselves with Asia as a kind of reaction. The dispute over the relative importance of Asia and Europe to American security was the main real issue of debate during the MacArthur controversy, with the case for regarding Asia rather than Europe as the centre of the world power-balance being argued in the General's evidence during the inquiry and the administration's rebuttal presented in the testimonies of Admiral Sherman and General Bradley.

However, one may observe in American attitudes to Asia not only a party difference, but a much greater general American willingness to intervene, to 'chance its arm', there than in Europe. It was the Asian half of the world crisis which led to American involvement in the second world war; an Asian issue, Korea, has been the only occasion since of major U.S. armed intervention; two other Asian crises—Indo-China and Formosa—have carried some of the most brusque war-bearing possibilities of recent years, and Vietnam at present is the only area where U.S. military personnel are involved in something close to combat. Historically, the lesser diffidence that Americans have shown in Asia than in Europe is not surprising, since until the rise of Japan Asia contained no power conceivably able to threaten U.S. security, and had none of the diplomatic prestige and sophistication of Europe. It held the golden promise of the China market— one of the oldest and most potent myths of international politics, still fairly effective—and offered an indefinite field for paternalistic 'do-gooding'. (It has often been pointed out that China was the U.S. version of the White Man's Burden, as India was Britain's.) The influence of China missionaries, or the sons of China missionaries, in the China Lobby and the U.S. foreign service is notable. Consciousness of the benevolence of American intention has injected a special element of resentment—a 'how sharper than a serpent's tooth' feeling into American attitudes to China ever since the traumatic events of 1949–50, which not only transformed China from friend and protégé to most bitter enemy, but brought many U.S. casualties at Chinese hands in the later stages of the Korean war. In terms of casualties, Korea has ranked only behind the first and second world wars among foreign wars for America.

The original point of difference between Britain and America on Asia in the post-war period, the question of recognition of the government in Peking, was a much less real cause of dissension at the time among policy-makers than it appeared. When Bevin decided on recognition late in 1949 he was motivated chiefly by consideration for the Commonwealth. He knew that India and Pakistan intended to recognize the new government, and that Australia and New Zealand did not, and he saw, rightly, that a split on purely racial lines on this question would make the Commonwealth look a rather dubious institution. (His avoidance of an undesirable colour solidarity then was paralleled by Canada's choice in the case of Suez.) There were other motives, of course. One was the position of Hong Kong, which could be seriously embarrassed by stopping supplies of water and food from the Chinese mainland. If China were given reason to try this and other forms of pressure there the situation of the Colony would rapidly become untenable. The hope for trade with China, and the possibility that British investments might be somehow safeguarded by diplomatic relations with the new government were influential, and so was the traditional British legal view that recognition is merely an acknowledgement of the fact of control rather than a gesture of approval. Finally, there was the consideration, usually suppressed in the cause of diplomatic tact and politeness, that British interests in China viewed Chiang Kai-shek with a great lack of enthusiasm. Not only did the British business community feel, perhaps naïvely, that conditions under a Communist government could hardly be worse than the disorder and inflation of the last days of the

Kuomintang, but the political and diplomatic demands that Chiang seemed likely to make—and to be supported by America—in the last days of the war offered an unpromising future for British interests. It will be recalled that Roosevelt at one point suggested that Churchill might agree to the handing over of Hong Kong as a sort of goodwill gesture. Churchill never at all shared Roosevelt's vision of China, restored to great power status, as a necessary part of the power-balance and a natural ally for the West in the post-war world. It is one of the ironies of recent history that America, which insisted on the creation of China's seat on the Security Council despite the reluctance of Britain and Russia, as a symbol of China's place as a great power, should later find herself fighting a longdrawn-out battle, against British and Russian pressure, to keep the actual government of China out of that seat. But though the State Department may have felt less than sympathetically inclined to some of the motivations of British policy, it did not in early 1950 regard with alarm or disapprobation the British intention of taking a step which would have been domestically uncomfortable for the American government at the time. In fact the State Department is said to have felt that the British recognition would be a useful trial balloon for American recognition. Acheson has plainly implied that the divergence of policy did not necessarily represent any breach of understanding[16] and there is reason to suppose that but for the entry of China into the war in Korea the State Department would have moved, with due caution, towards relatively early recognition.

The real dissensions came from late 1950 after the development of hostilities with China and the American non-receptiveness to Indian efforts to secure a place for itself in the peace-making process. From Attlee's flight to

[16] *Sketches from Life* (1961).

Washington at the end of 1950 in the fear (for which there was some evidence of justification) that America was about to become more heavily embroiled with China, through Eden's recalcitrance to Dulles's proposed line of action in Indo-China in 1954, and Britain's audible criticisms of American measures concerning Formosa, and Quemoy and Matsu, and the blunt dissociation from the line of American policy in Laos in 1958–61 (when it appeared directed to securing there the establishment of a right-wing rather than a neutralist government, as a potential ally), the general response of Britain to American initiatives has been a sceptical recalcitrance. In fact, if one had to base one's estimate of the strength of an alliance on the degree of consensus between the parties as to the nature and seriousness of the threat, and the proper technique to counter it, one might have difficulty in establishing the existence of an Anglo-American alliance in this part of the world at all, despite the formal legal tie of SEATO. SEATO is, in any case, all too obviously a far less coherent grouping than NATO, since it lacks not only the coalition army and command structure that is NATO's most distinctive feature, but the genuine sense of community of interest that informs NATO, whatever its tensions. Even as between the Asian members, for instance Pakistan and Thailand, such sense of common interests as exists is 'a sometime thing', easily dispersed by a differentiating Chinese policy, as with Pakistan in 1963.

Lack of consensus on either ends or means is also indicated by the fragmentary and bilateral character of the American alliance structure in the Pacific. America's treaty relations with Japan, South Korea, Formosa, the Philippines, Australia, and New Zealand are in effect separate undertakings by America to the minor powers concerned—they cannot be added up to a coherent entity because of the conflicts of these allies with each other, or

in their view of priorities. However, while one may note
the considerable resistances by Britain to American policy,
one must note also that Britain is, in the last analysis, unable to exert much independent power in the Pacific, and
has no alternative friend or ally there to replace America.
The limits of British ability to run any sort of alternative
policy to America were indicated as early as the 1920s,
when she relinquished the Japanese alliance at America's
behest. The positions of Australia and New Zealand underline the limits of British freedom of action. The foreign
policies of these two members of the Commonwealth are
essentially a process of reconciling the traditional British
tie with the reality of American power: as with Canada in
the same situation this results in uncomfortable tensions
wherever there is divergence between the Antipodean
powers' 'great and powerful friends', to use Sir Robert
Menzies's phrase. The discomfort has been demonstrated
rather more clearly in the Australian and New Zealand
cases than in the Canadian, through the existence of
ANZUS. But just as NATO resolved most of the difficulties
of Canadian foreign policy, so SEATO has eased some of
the difficulties of Australian and New Zealand policy. It
may be a less effective organization than NATO, but it
docs tend towards an alignment of Anglo-American policy
in Asia.

Most of the conflict between British and American
policy in Laos was resolved after 1961 by the resignation on the part of the Kennedy administration of any
ambitious views as to the potentialities of a right-wing
government there as an ally. On the other hand it is conceivable that some sort of military exigency resembling
that over Dien Bien Phu in 1954 in North Vietnam might
arise within a year or two in South Vietnam. (Indeed, it
is not only conceivable, it is beginning, despite the heavy
censorship, to look quite probable.) But such a military

emergency would not necessarily now produce a diplomatic crisis on the lines of that of 1954 between America and Britain. All five of the major powers involved in 1954 have altered their stances in the area. One of them, France, has a much diminished ability to intervene, though de Gaulle has indicated some remaining ambitions to play a hand there. America still regards the retention of the Western sphere of power in Vietnam as a vital national interest, but the military means likely to seem appropriate to the present administration is not the one that occurred to Dulles and Radford in 1954—that is, atomic strike. There has been a fairly complete reversion to notions of conventional and guerrilla warfare in such theatres of operations. Since the Vietnamese Communist Party is now under heavy Chinese influence, it is unlikely that Russia would make much effort or take many risks to help it attain power. How far China would be prepared to take risks that would enable her to pursue simultaneously its quarrels with America and with Russia must remain uncertain until the event. Britain would no doubt tend, as in 1954, to be reluctant to see the Western powers heavily involved in military action in so unpromising a terrain, but this incentive towards a compromise settlement must be somewhat offset by the fact that Australia and New Zealand (as members of SEATO), and Malaysia (for whose military defence Britain is still responsible), would be deeply alarmed and infuriated by any further territorial extension of the effective power of China, whether by military victory or diplomatic compromise. So that all in all a new military crisis in South Vietnam would now be less likely to produce a diplomatic conflict on 1954 lines between Britain and America than to sharpen the already existing diplomatic conflict between Russia and China. But the turn in the central power-balance since the beginning of 1963, which has given Russia an urgent

interest in the isolation of China, and which suggests that
the main theatre for the new cold war of the foreseeable
future may be the periphery of China (including the
Russian as well as the Indian border area), is likely to
provide a more demanding strategic and diplomatic role
for Britain, and perhaps a revival, after near desuetude,
of the notion of the Commonwealth as a serious security
alliance in South Asia. This is a point that will be developed later.

Relations outside Europe: the Middle East

If the Anglo-American alliance has had a rather
stunted and anaemic growth in East Asia, its mere
existence has been subject to doubt and to near-fatal con-
vulsions in West Asia, that is the Middle East. Even the
fragile tie of common formal membership of an alliance
can hardly be shown to exist, since the U.S. is a member
of CENTO only, so to speak, *sub rosa*. The first Middle
Eastern episode in which the two powers can be seen to be
taking joint action is their respective moves into Lebanon
and Jordan in 1958 after the Iraqi coup, hardly an episode
to reflect on with much satisfaction. Perhaps this has been
historically an extension of traditional British policy in the
area. Until very recently British reactions, in official and
commercial quarters concerned with the Middle East, to
the idea of active American intervention there has been at
best ambivalent and in many cases actively hostile, rather
like the mood in which American policy since the Monroe
Doctrine has regarded British influence in Latin America.
Ever since the late eighteenth century, one may say, the
dominant impulse in British policy in the Middle East had
been to exclude from that area the competitive intrusion
of any other great power. The great power most likely,
and geographically best placed, to challenge Britain was

always Russia, but there have been other European rivals for Britain's predominant position—the French, the Germans, even the Italians—and British policy has regarded each of them with more or less the same chilly disfavour that it has turned on Russian efforts at encroachment. At least this is how it has looked to the other powers concerned: the French for instance, including de Gaulle, have never ceased to believe that British officials diligently undermined their position in Syria and the Lebanon.

Has there been any particular reason why Britain should react more favourably to the increase of American interest and American power in the area than she did previously to the attempted increase of Russian, French, German, or Italian power? Certainly in its origins the American political entrance into the Middle East power arena was co-operative with Britain, in the context of the Middle East Supply Centre, Anglo-American from 1941, and concerned with the forwarding of goods to Russia through Iran. Even here co-operation was shot through with conflicts at a high policy level, conflicts which ultimately brought an end to the Centre.[17] Very substantial American oil interests had grown up in the Middle Eastern area, not much promoted or protected by the State Department, since the 1920s. America had by the early 1940s the dominant interest in Saudi Arabian oil, substantial interests in Kuwait and Bahrein, and shares also in the oil of Iran and other areas. While these oil interests had been originally sought for purely commercial reasons, their strategic and possible long-term economic value began to be realized during the 1940s as the proven reserves of America appeared to dwindle while those of the

[17] See the account given by the British Ambassador concerned, Sir Reader Bullard, in *The Camels Must Go* (pp. 247–65). Bullard implies that a major reason for British resentment was that America expected Britain to do the dirty work in the common security interest, as in the arrests of Zahedi and Kashani, then preached at them for doing so.

Middle East rose spectacularly. The great proponent within the American administration of the notion of Middle Eastern oil as a major American national interest was James Forrestal, as Secretary of the Navy and of Defence.[18]

The growth of American oil interests in the area could hardly fail to be attended by some friction with British interests, since these two groups were clearly each other's chief competitors. The world of the great oil companies is a discreet and heavily cartellized one, which watches its public relations carefully, and there have not been many overt political repercussions of these rivalries. But there was some murmuring in Britain, especially among Conservative back-benchers, at various aspects of American policy during the dispute between Britain and Iran over the nationalization of the Abadan refinery, and over the settlement which greatly diminished the degree of British control of Iranian oil and considerably enhanced that of the U.S. companies. And, of course, in the assorted British disputes with the King of Saudi Arabia over the Buraimi oasis (where the presence of oil was expected, apparently mistakenly) and over the Sultanate of Muscat and Oman, and the Gulf Sheikhdoms, there have been a good many *sotto voce* British reproaches directed at American policy. Such matters as the supply of arms and money to the King of Saudi Arabia and the lack of American efforts to restrain his adventures have produced an irritable Foreign Office conviction that the basic premise of American policy is that the King must be kept friendly at all costs, even if it means no visas for American Jewish servicemen, and no driving the family car for oil-company wives. However, considering the enormous size of the economic interests involved, the surprising thing is not that there has been some friction, but that there has been so little, and

[18] See *The Forrestal Diaries*.

that it has mostly been conducted in such hushed and discreet voices that few people have even been aware of its existence. Oil-men may cut each other's throats, but they do so in gentlemanly quiet.

Despite its growing economic interests in the area, a really large scale American post-war political involvement with a Middle Eastern issue did not occur until 1946, when Truman took the vital decision to back the government of Iran in its dispute with Russia over an oil concession that the Russians were demanding in Northern Iran, and in their efforts to secure the removal of the Russian troops, left over from the war in that area, and to end Russian support of an alleged 'autonomous government' in Azerbaijan. One must regard American policy here as showing a distinct and symbolic variation from traditional British policy, one which points to the nature of their general differences in the Middle East. Britain had tended, since the Anglo-Russian agreement of 1907, to tolerate in Iran a sharing of the field of influence with Russia, rather than to put up, as it were, a *first*-ditch resistance to it. The tacit agreement on spheres of influence, which can be held in some degree to have persisted in British policy even in Bevin's time, was certainly not inherited by America. The U.S. administration, prepared to take over with some diplomatic bluntness the traditional task of blocking the growth of Russian power in the area, clearly interpreted that task rather differently, drew the lines in somewhat different places, showed somewhat less sympathy for Russia's prickliness about the immediate vicinity of her southern border. But there was another and even more striking thing to note in this settlement. If America took a somewhat more intransigent line on the problem of the outside great power, she took a far more sympathetic view of the other force involved, that of local nationalism. How two-edged a victory by a small

D

power against a great power may be for another great power in the same area is clearly illustrated by comparing Dr Musadiq's attitude in the crisis with Russia in 1946, and in the later crisis with Britain over Abadan. In the earlier crisis he remarked that what Iran wanted was not a balance of Britain against Russia but a negative balance— i.e. neither Russian nor British influence, a notion he pursued with some zeal in the later crisis.

The chief apparent failure, both intellectual and moral, of Britain's external policy after 1945 has been inability to find a *modus vivendi* with Middle Eastern nationalisms. (Of course it may be maintained that this is one of those forces which allow no *modus vivendi*.) But whether the nationalists have been Israelis or Iranians, Egyptians or Jordanians, Iraqis or Kuwaitis, Yemenis or Adenites, policy formulation has hardly got beyond a series of shabby and rather unsuccessful rearguard actions. American policy had at least the advantage of a difference of moral viewpoint on the situations created by the clash of these nationalisms with the interests of the Western powers, and the great, violent, exemplification of that difference was, of course, Suez. One may concede that the difference in moral viewpoint arose primarily from the fact that the Americans had much less, relatively, at stake in the area: that it is easy to be virtuous about other nations' power interests. (In the only equivalent situation for America, the control of the Panama Canal zone, there is not much sign of a disinterested sympathy with the national feelings of the local people against the dominant great power of the area.) But this did not cancel out the original advantage of American diplomats, namely that they were not committed in anything like the same degree to the defence of inherited advantages and responsibilities, and were thus less involved in overt conflict with the local nationalists. What *did* cancel out this American advantage, or most of

it, was their special relation with the most resolute of all
the intransigent nationalisms of the area, that of the
Israelis.

The interconnectedness of British policy on Palestine
with American attitudes, dating from the days of the Bal-
four Declaration (which was made with an eye to the
American section of the Zionist movement) is one of the
more striking, though not one of the happier examples of
the two countries' relatedness. The horrifying human consequences of British efforts to turn back the stream of
refugees from Hitler's Europe towards Palestine, and the
series of shifts and devices by which Truman infuriated
Bevin (seeking to intervene, but refusing responsibility)—
these episodes display the decision-making processes in
Britain and America respectively at their characteristic
worst. The Middle East might have been regarded as the
one area in which Britain should find it easier to get along
with Republicans than with Democrats, if it were not
for Suez. Yet Dulles's Middle Eastern concept, called
successively the 'Northern Tier', the Baghdad Pact,
or CENTO, which seemed in 1953–4 to Israel to indicate U.S. deviation towards the Foreign Office's Arab-
oriented policy, contained in itself the seeds of the next
British disaster. For it was the quarrel with Egypt over
the recruitment of an Arab state, Iraq, to the Baghdad
Pact in 1955 that brought to its bitter end the apparently
hopeful new direction taken in 1954 in Anglo-Egyptian
relations, with the Churchill–Eden decision (at American
urging) to give up the Suez Canal base. The combination
of the possibility of nationalizing the Canal (offered by
the exit of the last British troops) and the incentive to pro-
claim defiance of the West in the name of Arab nationalism
provided by the degeneration of relations because of the
Baghdad Pact would probably have been too much for any
Arab leader to resist.

Of all the crises of post-war history, surely none was so inflated by illusion as the Suez adventure. Retrospectively it all seems to have had surprisingly little permanent effect, like one of those desert sandstorms which while they are going on obliterate every landmark and apparently portend the end of the world, but blown over, leave no more sign of their passing than a rearrangement in the pattern of the dunes. No doubt the cause of Arab nationalism was advanced, but President Nasser is still not undisputed master of the Middle East. No doubt the decay of British influence was speeded up, but the oil still flows, the Kuwaiti balances are still kept in London, and the Russians are not yet on the Persian Gulf. The Canal, that was to choke within months, has instead flourished economically and technically as never before. The Commonwealth, confidently diagnosed as never to be the same again, was in some respects more coherent in 1963 than it had been in 1955. Anglo-American relations, except for the scar-tissue on many Conservative hearts, were closer by 1957 than they had been before the crisis. But because Suez was the most violent single explosion in Anglo-American relations since the war, an account that played it down would be rather a case of Hamlet without Polonius —preferable, perhaps, but lacking authenticity. Even aside from the storm of public feeling, it is a crisis worth scrutinizing stage by stage for the illustration it offers of the natural limits of alliance, the way in which the policies of both parties were shaped by the conflict between national interest and the 'alliance' interest. Consolingly, it also may stand as evidence that an alliance able to recover from these events must have a good deal of natural stamina.

There are three stages at which one can see the conflict of national interest and the alliance interest: the initial decision to revoke the Aswan dam offer; the American

decision, after the nationalization of the Canal, to stall off
Anglo-French military action and to seek a compromise,
negotiated settlement; the American decision, after the
Anglo-French and Israeli military actions were launched,
not to allow the three powers to attain their military
objectives. Then there follows a fourth stage in which
national interests and the alliance interest again point in
the same direction, with the efforts to retrieve the damage
in the Western position resulting from the operation as a
whole.

It is in the first of these stages, the decision to revoke
the Aswan dam offer, or rather the decision as to how it
should be done, that American policy most deserves reproach for inadequate consideration of the possibilities,
as far as the allied interest was concerned. Dulles himself
has been somewhat too harshly blamed for the decision: it
was largely attributable to Congress (and to the lobbyists)
rather than the State Department. The best available
'inside' narrator of the events of the crises makes this clear.

But any attempt to give aid to the Arabs always met with
opposition behind the scenes in Washington. . . . Had the
members of Congress either underestimated or overlooked the
strength of such feeling they would have been quickly reminded
of it by the alert representatives of the many well-organized
pro-Israel lobbies that were always effective and influential in
the Capitol. . . . Congress, under continual pressure from
Israel's diplomatic and organization lobbies, was even more
fed up than Eisenhower and Dulles with Nasser's behaviour.
It was extremely doubtful if the President could have obtained
Congressional approval of the grants and loans to the Egyptians
at that point.[19]

[19] Sherman Adams, *Firsthand Report: the Story of the Eisenhower Administration* (1961), pp. 247–9. It is to be hoped that Adams, who believes Turkey,
Iran, and Pakistan to be Arab nations (see p. 249), did not represent the
degree of White House expertise on Middle Eastern questions at the time.
But there is no reason to doubt that he understood the domestic political
pressures on Dulles and Eisenhower.

Dulles's, however, was the decision to make the refusal as blunt as possible, more blunt than appears if one looks only at the official note. This in itself was unpleasant enough for an ambitious nationalist leader to receive, since it implied that Egypt was engaged on courses likely to lead to bankruptcy, and this statement was likely to damage President Nasser's prospects of raising funds abroad. But it was accompanied by one of those 'inspired leakages' that the State Department so often uses as instruments of policy, to the effect that President Nasser had now passed the point of no return in his relations with the Soviet Union, and that he and Egypt must therefore be considered as complete captives of the Kremlin.[20] The choice of this particular mode of breaking the bad news to Egypt was not as gratuitous or pointless as it appears. It was part of an attempt by Dulles to avert a double-edged threat to the whole basis of the American alliance system. The advent of an era of 'competitive coexistence' and 'positive neutralism' had brought with it the prospect of competitive diplomatic seduction: that is of the U.S. and Russia as, so to speak, rival 'protectors' competing for the favours of a bunch of gold-digging neutralists. Some of America's hard-bought Asian friends appeared to be wondering if they might not be able to make a better thing out of neutrality than out of alignment with the West. Dulles faced, therefore, two real threats to the American national interest as leader of a world-wide alliance system: on the one hand the possibility that Congress might be driven by such tactics to revolt against the aid programme in general; on the other hand America's allies might opt for the apparently more advantageous role of neutrals. He was worried enough about the growing prevalence of the idea that allies fared no better at American hands than neutrals to produce figures to prove the contrary early in

[20] See *New York Herald Tribune.* 25 Nov. 1956.

the year.[21] In these circumstances, the necessity of refusing the Aswan dam money came to seem a moment for demonstrating to the minor powers some of the difficulties they could get themselves into by such policies as Egypt's. When Dulles was asked in his press conference of 3 April 1957 whether the refusal had been in order to force a showdown with the Soviet Union in the Middle East, he said he thought that question could be answered in the negative; however, he went on to say

[the] issue was, do nations which play both sides get better treatment than nations which are stalwart and work with us? That question was posed by the manner in which the Egyptians presented their final request to us, and stalwart allies were watching very carefully to see what the answer would be; stalwart allies which included some in the same area.

Under all the circumstances, I think there was no doubt whatsoever as to the propriety of the answer given. . . . [22]

One may say therefore that the Aswan gambit was not unreasonable from the point of view of the American alliance system: the trouble was that it left out of calculation that President Nasser had within his grasp an interest important to the West as a whole and particularly to Britain and France. In the circumstances, it was bound to seem like a case of burning the house down—someone else's house—in order to keep America's soup warm. However, the British and French *locus standi* for reproach on this point would be a good deal better if they had not apparently, just as much as the Americans themselves, overlooked this possibility and encouraged Dulles to make the Aswan refusal as sharp as possible.[23]

The second stage of American policy was the decision, after the nationalization of the Canal, to use every possi-

[21] *New York Times*, 7 Mar. 1956.
[22] Ibid., 3 Apr. 1957.
[23] See Adams, pp. 247-9, on Eden's attitude at the beginning of 1956.

bility in the way of negotiation, diplomatic pressure,
manoeuvre, and delaying action in order to prevent or
postpone a resort to military force by Britain and France,
and to produce a negotiated settlement. The harshest
interpretation of this policy is to regard it as a matter of
domestic party advantage for Dulles and Eisenhower,
attributable to fear lest the outbreak of hostilities should
damage Eisenhower's electorally useful reputation as a
peacemaker, and lend colour to Democratic campaign
accusations that American foreign policy was in a bad
way. This would indeed, if it were the true American
motivation, be a case of sacrificing an ally to party advantage. But it is not a very plausible explanation of the
administration's line of policy. The Suez crisis, even if it
had earlier come to fighting, was not in itself of a nature to
disturb the President's popularity. Suez is a long way from
America, the issue was a remote one to most Americans.
The only substantial number of electors emotionally
involved in the situation were the friends of Israel, whose
votes are normally committed to the Democrats and could
have been won for the Republicans only by strong anti-
Nasser policies. The inhibition against putting in a new
President at a time of crisis was bound to favour Eisenhower, and was more effective at the time of the election
than Democratic criticisms of Republican foreign policy.
All in all, if the administration's choice had been made
purely on a vote-getting basis, a much harsher line towards
President Nasser would have been indicated.

Dulles's decision that Britain and France must be discouraged by all the considerable resources at his command
from the effort at a military settlement is attributable
rather to three other factors: the moral judgement that
this was not a situation in which the use of force was justi-
fiable; the calculation that permitting such an effort at
the use of force would rally the Arab-Asian powers around

President Nasser and would increase the deep distrust of Western purposes among the Asian neutrals; and a certain degree of instinctive anti-colonialism. By the standards of Roosevelt or Cordell Hull the anti-colonialism of Eisenhower and Dulles was mild enough, but a general slight distrust of the European powers as uncertainly-reformed burglars who might stray back into their old ways is part of the normal framework of the American mind on this matter. In Dulles's case the feeling emerged quite clearly in a couple of his characteristic stumblings of phrase in press conferences.

Aside from the question of whether the judgements of the American national interest and of the moral relationships of the issue were reasonable ones, one must ask whether the American mode of putting them into effect was well considered. *Prima facie*, the answer must be no, since after all the policy was unsuccessful, in that an attempt at a solution by force *was* made. The fact that the most powerful country on earth was unable to restrain two relatively dependent allies and a semi-pensioner from a course of action that it disapproved of is in itself an indictment of sorts against American diplomatic method, though also a kind of tribute. Here perhaps the fatal factor in the situation was less the relation of Britain to America than the relation of Eden to Dulles. The true mystery of the Suez adventure is how so experienced a diplomatist as Eden miscalculated the political context of the military action so far as to believe it would be successful. If he was misled about the American attitude, if he believed that the U.S. government, though disapproving, would remain neutral, would temporize until it could be presented with a *fait accompli*, and would keep the Russians from interfering, then his judgement that the action could succeed becomes reasonable. If Dulles, either consciously or unconsciously, let Eden fall into this error, it would be a heavy count against his efficiency as a diplomatist. There is the famous though apocryphal story that Dulles's first question to the first British Embassy official he saw after the crisis was 'Why on earth didn't you push through with it?' Doubtless this reflects an embittered British feeling that they had been led to expect acquiescence in a *fait accompli*, and had then been confronted by something very different. But the Americans might retort that there was no *fait accompli* for them to accept, that so slow-motion an invasion was diplomatically impossible to acquiesce in. In any case, even if troops had been placed along the Canal fairly rapidly, there is no reason to believe the matter would have been thus satisfactorily concluded. 80,000 British troops were based along the Canal in the period up to the evacuation agreement of 1954, and the situation then was judged not worth its costs.

One of the main reasons for U.S. resentment of British and French policy was their belief that it was premised on an assumption that America must 'pick up the check' if Russia intervened: that is save Britain and France from the possible consequences of their own policies despite any nuclear risks such a rescue operation would involve for America. This calculation does not in fact seem to have been made in Whitehall: there simply was no belief in any Russian intention of intervening. The possibility was taken more seriously in Washington, or so one would judge from a speech by Douglas Dillon, the U.S. Ambassador in Paris, and the fact that Eisenhower ordered a general alert. But even if there was never any chance of Russian military intervention, there was a sense in which the Suez adventure did force America to pick up the check against Russian diplomatic advance in the development of its Middle Eastern policy from 1957. To allow Russia to monopolize the role of 'the Arabs' friend', or to allow the Afro-Asian powers generally to assume that the West was all tarred with the same imperialist brush was a supposition that would have greatly endangered the viability of those governments, such as Iran, that had aligned themselves with the West. If Dulles had chosen this course he might have preserved his allies, Britain and France, from a heavy diplomatic defeat, and seen them back in something like the pre-1954 situation on the Canal, but only at heavy risk to his alliances elsewhere. Moreover, even if there had been a credit balance on such a transaction, it would have had to be set against other disadvantages of allowing the military action to go on. Another defeat at the hands of the West would not precisely have helped the emergence of moderate or right-wing forces in Egypt. The history of nationalist movements in other areas, Indo-China or Algeria or Indonesia, is that the longer they are in the wilderness or under arms the more leadership tends to shift to the left, so that a movement uniting a whole spectrum of political opinion, including some Communists, ends by a process of subversion or conspiracy or attrition under strong Communist influence.

When the dust had settled, the main damage to the Western alliance from the events of November 1956 was seen to be the crumbling of the British sphere of influence in the Middle East. Even before the Suez adventure this sphere of influence had been only the shell of its former self, but it had produced an effect from a distance. The destruction of the 1954 treaty arrangement whereby Britain was entitled to reactivate the Suez base in the event of attack on Egypt or other Arab League countries was of some moment. The new 'forward' American policy in the Middle East, symbolized by the Eisenhower Doctrine, which was brought into being to make good this damage, ought perhaps to be regarded chiefly as a declaration of intentions, a notification to Russia, and even more to Congress, of the new sphere of direct American interest, and a morale-stiffener for those forces among the Arabs which might otherwise have seen themselves with no powerful friend in the world.

One aspect of the Suez crisis which tended to be overlooked at the time but was to prove symptomatic later was its illustration of the lines of cleavage in the ambiguous triangular relation between Britain, France, and America. (Triangular ever since 1778 in the sense of Britain and France as 'alternative friends' for America, and lately triangular with America and France as 'alternative friends' for Britain.) Britain remained, save for those few wild days of early November, basically amenable to American pressure, partly no doubt because in her vulnerable situation as regards external balances there was no real alternative, partly because of the 'meta-diplomatic' aspects of the relationship with America. France was not in anything like the same degree responsive to pressure: for her the Suez adventure ended not because the Americans or the U.N. disapproved, but because the British feebly gave way to American arm-twisting. Similarly, the breach in the alliance was far less rapidly and explicitly mended, as far as France was concerned, the Eisenhower Doctrine was far less well received, no French equivalent developed to the Anglo-American co-operation in CENTO, or to the joint (or, as people used to say over Suez, collusive) landings in the Lebanon and Jordan in 1958 after the Iraqi coup. One might regard this period as indicating British acceptance, even in the Middle East, of the role of junior partner to American power.

In part the differences between British and French attitudes in the aftermath of Suez must be put down to the corroding effects of the war in Algeria, which at this time was approaching its cruellest point. But the greater recalcitrance of France than Britain towards American policy in relations with the Arab world is one example of a general divergence. This is visible even before Macmillan succeeded Eden as Prime Minister, in the sense of urgency with which the repair of the alliance was regarded in Westminster. There was no French counterpart to Eden's desperate effort, of which Sherman Adams has given an account, to see Eisenhower in November or December. As to the meeting that was in due course arranged, at Bermuda in March, one may indubitably put a good deal down to Macmillan's bland unawareness of difficulties. The political technique of picking one's way through a minefield in the apparent conviction that one is sauntering at ease in broad and flowery meadows no doubt has its diplomatic uses, and the philosophical acceptance of conflict and defeat within the alliance is at least a way of establishing its non-frangible quality, if a somewhat painful one for British sensibilities.

2

Balance in Motion

THE years 1957 and 1958 mark the end of the first epoch, not merely the first decade, of the cold war, the beginnings of transformation in the power alignments that had shaped world politics since the Truman Doctrine. The essential characteristic of that power-balance had been its bipolarity. The obvious milestone of 1957 was, of course, the first Russian sputnik, and what it indicated for relationships on the Western side of the balance. Only quite recently has it become clear that the impact of this event, in a less direct way, was even more important on the Communist side of the balance, in what it was to contribute to the schism between Russia and China over diplomatic strategy in relation to the non-Communist world. The obvious event of 1958 was the death of the Fourth Republic and the re-accession to power of General de Gaulle, with what these indicated for the future direction of Europe; the now half-forgotten aspect of this year was the renewal of Berlin crisis by Khrushchev in a form that provided a wedge potentially to divide Germany from America. An event less dramatic than these, the agreement of October 1957 between Eisenhower and Macmillan on co-operation in nuclear weapons, represented a quasi-renewal of the 'special relationship' that had existed between Britain and America in this field until 1946, and was to help ensure that in any choice between America and 'Europe', Britain would choose the American connexion.

New stage in advanced weapons

Let us look first at the last event, the new turn in Anglo-American relations in advanced weapon systems. The 1955 British White Paper on defence policy had announced the intention of building British nuclear weapons: the first of them was tested in May 1957. The decision may be regarded as based on a 'counterforce' strategy (later abandoned, but now perhaps being retrieved) in the sense that the main military justification (as against political or diplomatic ones) for a nuclear strike-force specifically under British control, and usable in accordance with a British scheme of priorities rather than an alliance or American scheme of priorities, was that it might be used against targets whose knocking out would be vital to the survival of Britain, but less vital to the alliance as a whole. Such targets would, obviously, be air bases (and later rocket bases) from which strikes seemed likely to be directed at targets in Britain. (The question of relative priorities in targeting, sometimes dismissed as of no real account, seems rather more relevant when one considers it in the light of a past actual instance. The V1 and V2 rocket bases in North-Eastern Europe in the closing stages of the second world war were a comparatively low-priority target from the point of view of the overall military purposes of the Western alliance, since the rockets did little actual military damage. But this is hardly the light in which they appeared to the inhabitants of southern England, and in fact the British government, having its own strike-force, was able to devote rather more of it to destroying them than was called for in strict military logic. The potential conflict between alliance interest and national interest in the disposition of air forces was illustrated even more strikingly by the British decision in 1940 to withold fighter aircraft for the defence of Britain itself rather than use them against the Germans in France. The whole Battle of Britain turned on this choice.) The shorter the war envisaged, the more important relative priorities in targeting would be. Churchill put it thus:

... we cannot be sure that in an emergency the resources of other Powers would be planned exactly as we would wish, or that the targets which would threaten us most would be given what we consider the necessary priority, or the deserved priority, in the first few hours.[1]

However, though this sharp military incentive to an independent strike-force was of course mentioned in the debate over the H-bomb decision, most of the argument in March 1955 turned on the question of British diplomatic influence, especially with America, and the degree to which it might be reduced by a British acceptance of a situation of total dependence on the U.S. in this field. These decisions were taken before the growth in Soviet delivery systems, symbolized by the sputnik, had begun to cast more than a fraction of the later shadow of doubt on the credibility of the American deterrent for the safety of America's allies (as against America itself). But well before British nuclear weapons actually began to pass into the country's stockpiles in substantial numbers (probably early 1958) a considerable revision of expectations and strategic concepts was under way. At this time, late 1957 to early 1958, the V-bomber force was reaching its peak effectiveness, the two later models of aircraft, the Victor and Vulcan, having better heights and speeds than the chief American delivery vehicle of the time, the B-52. Yet weapons-development decisions must be taken with the situation of five years hence in mind, and already the manned strategic bomber was beginning to look a good deal less convincing for the foreseeable future than mis-

[1] H. C. Deb., 5th ser., 1 Mar. 1955, vol. 537, col. 897.

siles of various ranges. At the Bermuda meeting of March
1957 between Macmillan and Eisenhower (the post-Suez
meeting) it was agreed that American guided missiles
should be available to Britain. The missiles concerned
were the Thors, whose installation was completed (60 missiles, each with a two-megaton warhead) in 1958. The
installation of these missiles may be interpreted either as
part of the post-Suez British effort to build deterrent
forces, or as part of the American effort to counter the
growth of Soviet rocket strength. No doubt it partook of
both, but in view of the timing of the original decision,
before the sputnik, the former element was probably the
more important. In terms of Anglo-American strategic
relations, it represented a growth of British influence, or
at any rate British veto-power, as compared to the SAC
bases, since the Thor missiles were subject to control on
the 'two-keys' system—that is, they could only be fired if
a British officer, acting on instructions from Downing
Street, as well as an American officer, acting on instructions from the White House, operated their respective
elements in the mechanism. On the other hand, they were
more clearly a Russian first-strike target than even the
SAC bases, because of the greater probability that they
could be knocked out completely on the ground, and the
negligible probability that anything could be done about
the missiles once they were fired.

The March agreement on the Thor missiles was a preliminary to more far-reaching agreement of October 1957
(at a meeting in Washington of Eisenhower and Macmillan) which restored something like the pre-McMahon
Act degree of collaboration between Britain and America
in nuclear research. As far as Britain was concerned,
access to American atomic information had already proceeded almost *pari passu* with the growth of her own knowledge of nuclear technology. A 1954 amendment to the

E

McMahon Act (consequent on the 'Atoms for Peace' programme) had permitted a good deal of preferential treatment for Britain by administrative arrangement. In 1956,
just before the Suez crises, there had been an American
agreement to provide information helpful for the building
in Britain of an atomic reactor for service in a submarine
engine, a vital development in view of the later decision
on the Polaris missile as the main carrier of the British
nuclear warheads. It meant that the building of a British
squadron of nuclear-powered submarines was quite
feasible in 1963, in marked contrast to the situation in
France.

The dependence of the liberalizing of the McMahon
Act on independent research work was heavily underlined
in the hearings on the change. Access was to be confined to
those nations which have

achieved considerably more than a mere theoretical knowledge
of atomic weapons design, or the testing of a limited number
of atomic weapons. It is intended that the co-operating nation
must have achieved a capability of its own of fabricating a
variety of atomic weapons, and constructed and operated the
necessary facilities, including weapons research and development laboratories, weapons manufacturing facilities, a weapon
testing station, and trained personnel to operate each of these
facilities.[2]

In 1958 there could be no doubt that this restricted the
operation of the amendment to Britain. Up to August
1963 it was still interpreted to exclude France, since France
had until then tested only 'a limited number of atomic
weapons'. One may say that the principle 'to him that
hath shall be given' has been the operative one as far as
atomic secrets are concerned. That is, access has been
possible only when the traffic is potentially two-way. One

[2] Report of the Joint Committee on Atomic Energy, 85th Congress, 2nd
sess., Senate Report 1654, p. 12.

can undoubtedly maintain that this aspect of Anglo-American relations acted as a direct incentive to France to buy her way into the Western nuclear club, and that for instance Italy might be regarded as subject to the same incentive (Germany is in a different case, not so much because of the fragile legal restrictions of WEU as because of the real diplomatic impediments to her freedom of action.) Yet it is difficult to see that any other criterion was likely to be used, unless one is supposing a world in which nationalist feelings were considerably diminished. For the advantages of the nuclear oligopoly to the dominant powers are so real, and the dangers to themselves of nuclear diffusion are so genuine, that neither Russia nor America has been likely freely to endow any ally with this potentiality for damage to its own position. On the other hand, where nuclear power already exists independently, the case is entirely altered, for then one is not creating a danger (the danger is already there) but making a bargain. This factor, which one might call 'nuclear egotism', has thus operated on balance to restrict the membership of the nuclear club, not to increase it. It has meant that none of the nuclear powers has been prepared to pay the entry fee of a minor power to the club: entry has thus been restricted to those prepared and able to pay the fee themselves. And not many powers either are or will be economically or politically in this position.[3] So one may say that the absence of any tendency to 'nuclear altruism' on the part of America, Russia, and Britain has no doubt operated to impel France and China towards building their own nuclear weapons, but it has also tended to make improbable the nightmare vision of atomic weapons in the hands of Rumania or Indonesia, Pakistan or Thailand, Guatemala or Egypt. (One trusts that the French will also prove

[3] See Leonard Beaton and John Maddox, *The Spread of Nuclear Weapons* (1962).

sufficiently lacking in nuclear altruism for this to continue
true of say, Israel and West Germany.)

However, as Beaton and Maddox have pointed out, the
differential degree of American assistance as between
Britain and France in the construction of advanced weapon
systems did not depend solely on their respective individual
levels of nuclear technology.

In truth, the issue is overwhelmingly political: the United
States will not at present share its atomic secrets with any
country which it can imagine using them in circumstances
which it would not approve. However the issue may be blurred
by diplomacy, the Americans trust the British far more than
they trust the French. This was probably increased rather
than decreased by Suez, the one major break in Anglo-
American relations since 1941. For it was then the British
accepted, in humiliation, the fact that in the face of American
opposition they could not go on. France did nothing of the
kind; nor have the French over the years been prepared to
give the Americans the same free hand on their territory as
Britain has done. This became public when in 1960 American
fighter-bombers had to be moved to Britain and Germany to
permit their re-equipment with nuclear weapons; but on day
to day matters it has been obvious to both governments for
years.[4]

The closeness of American–British relations in the tech-
nological-strategic field was not confined to the technology of actual bombs and warheads. The impediments
that deter countries other than the two dominant powers
from mounting a major power of nuclear strike (as
against making a few bombs, which is within the technical capacity of perhaps a dozen powers) is the expense
and the attainments in sophisticated technologies necessary for the means of delivery and efforts at defence
(planes, submarines, missiles). In these fields also the

[4] Ibid., p. 55.

preferential treatment of Britain has been marked. Even the Blue Streak engine, though developed by Rolls Royce, owed a good deal to an original American design. More important, in the reactor design for nuclear submarines, in which America had obtained a very notable lead with the Nautilus, the speed of British development of the Dreadnought, on which the whole question of Polaris was to turn, depended a great deal on the agreement reached with America in 1957 on marine nuclear engines.

But if Britain at this period was beginning to revert almost to a pre-McMahon Act relationship with America, Europe as a whole was being nudged one degree towards a pre-Marshall Plan stance, or at any rate the Carolingian impulse in Europe began to look more likely to prove dominant over the Atlantic one than had been the case since 1947. To understand why this was the case one must return to 1955.

New stage in Europe

The EDC fiasco was no doubt responsible for the somewhat casual and uninterested attitude adopted by British opinion towards the Messina initiative in 1955, in that it encouraged a placid assumption that this new start would probably not come to anything much either. Even after it had become apparent (by 1956) that it might come to something fairly considerable in the commercial field, and that Britain would do well to improve her own ability to bargain on tariffs, not much interest was taken in the diplomatic or strategic possibilities of the new arrangements. Thus the announcement in July 1956 of the British proposals for a European Free Trade Area, to be associated with the Common Market, seemed to indicate merely that Britain was interested in sharing the economic sugar, without swallowing the political pill. Almost the whole of the debate about the Free Trade Area and the EEC and their relative advantages for Britain between 1956 and 1961 was conducted in terms of economic loss or gain, just as later the project of full membership of the Common Market was mostly sold to British opinion, at least at the man-in-the-street level, on the basis of the economic growth-rate of Continental Europe (which was impressive but irrelevant since it proceeded chiefly from causes that had nothing to do with the Common Market). This was natural enough, in fact inevitable in view of the general consensus of British feeling on the matter, but it distracted attention from the changes in the diplomatic significance of Europe which began to be tentatively apparent from 1957–8.

In part the increased emphasis on the diplomatic aspect of the European movement since 1958 is a testimonial to de Gaulle's personal impact on world politics. Originally it might perhaps have been expected that his tenure of office would mark a dangerous setback to the whole idea of European integration, for he had always been suspicious not only of supra-national but even of any international arrangements which might impede France's freedom of action. (His attitudes to the U.N. and NATO are too well known to need dwelling upon.) Moreover, he had been one of the most dangerous enemies of the EDC, his first Prime Minister, Debré, had a solidly anti-European voting record in the Assembly, and his Foreign Minister, Couve de Murville, was a devoted Gaullist seemingly content to attend to the technicalities and not heckle on matters of policy.

That the actual turn of events proved so different may be regarded as a notable demonstration of the strength of the balance-of-power principle in international politics, operating in this case *within* the Western alliance, but subtly and intricately connected with the operation of the

balance *outside* the alliance, between the Western world
and Russia. It would be putting it rather crudely to say
that President de Gaulle envisaged using Germany to
balance against 'the Anglo-Saxons' within the NATO
alliance, just as he once envisaged using Russia in the
same role outside it. But in his general project of maximiz-
ing French diplomatic weight, that is restoring France to
the status of a 'great power', he has had two main instruments: the acquisition of a French nuclear force, and
France's special position as the leader and voice of Europe.
The way in which these two assets buttress each other will
be examined later. To look first at the 'leader-of-Europe'
asset, the most obvious thing about it is that as long as
Britain remains outside Europe, it depends essentially on
the tacit support of Germany, the only other obvious contender for the role. That is, France's bid for restored status
as a great power depended essentially on the acquiescence,
within Europe, of Dr Adenauer in French policies. And
interestingly enough it was Khrushchev who provided the
issue that promoted this acquiescence. Again it might
be classed as one of those coincidences that amount to
historic events that Khrushchev chose to renew the Berlin
crisis in November 1958, six months after the death of the
Fourth Republic, and just as de Gaulle found himself confirmed in his tenure of power by the elections of that
month and by the French acceptance of the constitution of
the Fifth Republic. For the Berlin crisis in its successive
spasms from November 1958 was undoubtedly the issue
round which the balance of power (or perhaps one should
say the balance of alignments) of 1958–63 within NATO
revolved. This balance was distinctly different from the
one which had prevailed during Dulles's tenure of office,
when there was a close rapprochement between Germany
and America, with most of the other NATO powers, led
by Britain and including France, somewhat apprehensive

about the potentialities of this so-called 'Washington–Bonn axis'. That particular set of alignments owed something to the personal friendship between Dulles and Adenauer, but objective factors of diplomatic interest also promoted it. The revival of the Berlin issue at the end of 1958, just as his mortal illness was slackening Dulles's hold on the reins of policy, produced a major modification of these alignments. For the recognition-of-East-Germany issue that has been intrinsically involved in any effort to ease the Berlin situation is the question on which the greatest natural divergence exists between the diplomatic interest of Germany and the diplomatic interests of the rest of the Western alliance. Even Dulles's attitudes on this question were not always pleasing to Adenauer: he was furious with some of the American proposals of late 1958 to early 1959. The only Western statesman prepared fully to endorse Adenauer's intransigence, in respect to East Germans as 'agents' of Russia, was de Gaulle, who was equally at this time looking for an ally inside the alliance. It is of course possible to put the French attitude as much down to de Gaulle's temperament as to diplomatic calculation, but whichever it was one may regard it as creating the Franco-German diplomatic mutual-aid society which was to stand him in good stead.

Other reasons than the signature of the Treaty of Rome and the death of the Fourth Republic make a case for regarding the years 1957–8 as marking a new turn in world politics, a logical end of the epoch that began with the Truman Doctrine in 1947. The essential characteristic of that ten-year period, the bipolarity of the balance of power, had been the basis of the hardly-questioned acceptance of continuing West European diplomatic dependence on America. In the decade 1947–57 the only concept of Western Europe that stood up to an examination of the strategic and political and economic realities had been the Atlantic concept. After so long a period in which this was the case, it took some time to re-establish the habit of considering whether it was any longer so. Yet the decisive factor of the immediate post-war years, the economic prostration of Europe, had vanished well before 1957. Even the apparent vulnerability of Europe to economic movements originating in America (which used to be celebrated in the phrase current in 1953–4, 'When America sneezes, Europe catches pneumonia') had been disproved by events. The successive period of mild recession in America did not put much of a crimp in the continuous European boom of the 1954–62 period, and if the boom did seem to be losing some afflatus by 1962 this did not seem to be connected with American causes.

Once the post-war economic recovery of Western Europe had reached this point, the chief reason why it remained unlikely to operate as an autonomous force in international politics was its continuing military weakness, both in the conventional and in the nuclear field. In essence the defence of Europe continued to rest simply on the credibility of the American guarantee, institutionalized in NATO, but to be implemented outside NATO through the nuclear striking force of SAC and its adjutants—a force directly under the control of the U.S. President, with NATO as such having no say as to its use. But by 1957 in this field also the situation was considerably different from the dark days of 1947–8 when the habit of dependence was first acquired. To look first at the conventional-forces side of the situation, France alone at that time was maintaining almost as large an army as America had at the end of the Eisenhower administration, 812,000 men as against 870,000, with a population a quarter the size. And Germany was reaching towards her planned NATO target of twelve divisions, a division-count larger than that available to Kennedy on his inauguration. In

fact by 1958, despite Britain's reductions of her armed
forces, the situation in respect of conventional forces potentially available on the Continent, had changed markedly
in favour of the European NATO powers, partly through
the growth of the German army and partly through the
prospect of an end of the war in Algeria sending the
French army home. If the political will had existed (which
admittedly was a very large proviso), there might have
appeared by that time not much reason why the long-
standing military aspiration of NATO (thirty divisions on
the central front) should not be turned into reality from
European sources only.

These forces, then called the 'shield' force of NATO,
were, of course, only the lesser part of the mechanism
created to discourage any Soviet inclination towards
adventures in Europe: the more important part was the
American (and in much lesser degree the British) power
of strategic nuclear strike. Even taking the most optimistic
view of probable British and French attainments, and
assuming some form of joint force, it remained unlikely
that Western Europe could mount more than 10 per cent
of American strike-power. And Europe must remain at an
insuperable disadvantage in the nuclear age, as compared
with Russia and America, because of its comparatively
small and closely-settled area, which must always make it
less able to survive nuclear attack or disperse nuclear
weapons than either of the other two. Though the problem of dispersal could possibly be offset by the use of a sea-
based delivery system such as Polaris, the problem of close
settlement would remain irreducible. And in any case
Europe was technologically backward in sophisticated
weapons systems such as rockets and nuclear submarines.

These considerations were all valid enough, and no
doubt provided strong reasons for assuming as an item of
faith, as the British did (and as the author very strongly

does) that the advantages of the American guarantee to Europe were and would remain far more valuable than almost any interest that Europe could promote by sacrificing them. Adhering to this view, one is a little inclined to underrate the strength of the case that could be put together to the opposite effect—the diplomatic and strategic case for Carolingian Europe. De Gaulle has, of course, made this case, but when it is clothed in the splendid obscurity of his rhetorical purple, its essential features tend to escape scrutiny.

The case turns largely on the possibility, or even probability, of a divergence of *strategic* interest between America and Western Europe, and once again the 1957–8 period marks a point of change. The bluntest expression of this potential divergence of interest between America and Russia on the one hand, and Europe (both East and West) on the other is in de Gaulle's press conference of 10 November 1959.

Who can say that if the occasion arises, the two [the U.S.A. and Russia], while each deciding not to launch its missiles at the main enemy . . . will not crush the others [the allies]? It is possible to imagine that on some awful day Western Europe would be wiped out from Moscow and Central Europe from Washington?[5]

This cannot altogether be dismissed as a flight of military fancy on the General's part. One of the less-examined implications of the debate on the relative usefulness of strategic nuclear weapons as against tactical atomic weapons was that the strategic weapons would be used by the two dominant powers directly against the centres of power and main bases of the other: that is to say against SAC and rocket bases chiefly in America and England, or Russian bases in the USSR. But in the case of tactical

[5] *New York Times*, 11 Nov. 1959.

atomic weapons, the area of use would be the area of the
land battle (that is Germany east and west of the line of
division) and the lines-of-communication area for each
side (that is, chiefly France for the NATO powers and
Poland for the Warsaw Pact). To put it at its harshest, the
choice between strategic and tactical weapons for each of
the dominant powers could be held to be a choice between the grievous prospect of devastation at home and
the somewhat less grievous prospect of the devastation of
their respective allies. And as their air-atomic power grew
more and more equal, their mutual advantage in choosing
tactical-atomic warfare also grew more equal. Back in
1954 Dulles could enlarge on 'massive retaliation' (i.e. the
strategic use of nuclear weapons) as a sufficient sanction
in itself for Western security, but by the late 1950s the
chief drive for the creation of the armies necessary for
tactical-atomic or conventional warfare was coming from
America, and the 'heel-dragging' in this matter was that of
the European powers. Some British and American comment has been inclined to treat the West German and
French lack of enthusiasm for the new turn in American
military policy as though this were merely inexplicable
wrong-headedness on the part of their leaders. But, after all,
though tactical-atomic weapons may seem less dangerous
to the world as a whole (assuming no 'escalation') than
strategic nuclear ones, for the people in the area of use the
distinction between Hiroshima-sized atomic bombs used
'tactically' against the railway junctions or port installations of a city, and a nuclear bomb used 'strategically'
against the city itself is likely to seem academic. And there
is also the consideration that to lighten the shadow of
possible destruction *for America and Russia themselves as
against their allies* must be to ease the inhibitions on the
actual decision-makers, who are at present all Americans
or Russians.

This restriction of the decision-making function, as far as the West is concerned, to America, was the root of de Gaulle's grudge against NATO, as he has made quite clear.

> ... the alliance was set up upon the basis of integration, that is to say, of a system whereby the defence of each of the countries of Continental Europe—not counting England—does not have a national character; a system in which, in fact, everything is under the command of the Americans and in which the Americans decide on the use of the principal weapons—that is to say, atomic weapons.[6]

In this particular quotation he has excepted Britain from the proposition that the European members of NATO had lost the power of decision in matters affecting their own security and were thus placed in a position of insulting national inferiority. But at other times, as in the press conference of May 1962, he has blandly assumed that there is no difference between the British position and that of the other European members. This may be a matter merely of mood or tactics on de Gaulle's part, but it may reflect his appreciation of a certain ambivalence in the British position. Britain, as has been pointed out, has adhered to the Atlantic concept of Europe throughout the post-war period, with not even so much as a glance towards the Carolingian concept, but all the same some elements of British policy have carried the suppressed premise that there might develop a divergence of strategic interest between America and Britain. In fact, this might be called the premise behind the whole of the British advanced-weapons programme, from Attlee's first decision to build atomic bombs. One of the few occasions of its being put into words was Duncan Sandys's defence of the decision to build the hydrogen bomb, in 1957:

[6] Press Conference, 5 Sept. 1960 (quoted *Nato Letter*, Nov. 1960, p. 24).

So long as large American forces remain in Europe, and American bombers are based in Britain, it might conceivably be thought safe . . . to leave to the United States the sole responsibility for providing the nuclear deterrent. But when they have developed the 5,000 mile inter-continental ballistic rocket, can we really be sure that every American Administration will go on looking at things in quite the same way.[7]

This particular potential divergence of strategic interest is quite a different one from that foreseen by General de Gaulle, but then this quotation dates from a different stage of the arms balance, before the vital swing symbolized by the Soviet sputnik of October 1957 had occurred. What was militarily important was not the sputnik itself but what the lapse of time between this Soviet success and an equivalent American success indicated as to the present and, even more, the future uncertainty about the outcome of the technological race between America and Russia. That the American lead in military technology, which seemed in 1945 almost immeasurable, should have given way only twelve years later to even a temporary and uncertain American inferiority in one related field marks the most important single movement in the post-war balance of power. Though the so-called 'missile gap', so much debated in 1959–60, has been heavily discounted since the Democratic administration came to power, this longer-term change in the technological balance cannot be discounted, nor can its implication of ambiguity as to the relative technological advantage of America or Russia for the foreseeable future. That it was not in fact discounted in Washington is indicated by the very considerable changes in American military policy after the advent to power of President Kennedy—especially by the increase of the American army from eleven to sixteen divisions, the wide powers obtained by the President to call up extra men, and

[7] 16 Apr. 1957, H. C. Deb., vol. 568, coll. 1760–1.

the choice of General Maxwell Taylor, the most eminent military enemy of the 'massive-retaliation' concept, first as President Kennedy's personal military adviser, and later as Chairman of the Joint Chiefs of Staff.

3

The 'Managed' Balance

The 'Kennedy changes'

HOWEVER, the 'Kennedy changes' were important in more than the strategic context. Few lines of comment, surely, have ever shown more complete misunderstanding of the processes which shape American foreign policy than the view widely expressed in the British press at the time of his accession to power that the departure of Eisenhower from office would mean a diminution in the closeness of relations between Britain and America. If the alliance had depended even in a marginal way on two elderly statesmen being able to reminisce about life in North Africa together during the war, it would indeed have been a fragile structure. In fact, personal relations between the chief American foreign-policy decision-maker and his British interlocuteurs were about as bad during much of the Republican administration as they have ever been this century. The advent of President Kennedy and his advisers (despite some frictions) represented a considerable gain in personal relations at most political consulting levels. For the decisive Republican foreign-policy maker was not Eisenhower but Dulles, and his English counterpart for the crucial part of the period was Eden. Contemplating the personal relationships between the two men can only make one conscious that if the alliance structure could survive the conflict between them, it has not much to fear from any readily foreseeable permutation in the President–Secretary of State–Prime Minister–Foreign Secretary quadrille.

It may be objected that this view dismisses Eisenhower's influence in too cavalier a fashion, but the evidence for it is provided by a first-hand observer endeavouring to make the opposite case, Sherman Adams. The portrait that emerges from between his ardently Republican lines of Dulles's manoeuvrings to maintain his own sphere of power has a certain historic comedy that entitles it to be presented without comment.

Eisenhower deferred to the tougher stand of Dulles in foreign policy because he agreed with his Secretary of State that the United States had to be more positive in its dealing with the Communists. . . . 'With my understanding of the intricate relationships between the peoples of the world, and your sensitiveness to the political considerations involved, we will make the most successful team in history' Dulles had prophesied. . . . Dulles saw to it that nobody but himself talked with Eisenhower about major policy decisions. He was in the White House more than any other Cabinet member, and he was the only government official who frequently spoke with the President on the telephone. . . . From time to time Dulles found in his diplomatic domain such presidential assistants as Harold Stassen, . . . Lewis Strauss . . . , C. D. Jackson . . . , Clarence Randall and Joseph Dodge. . . . Dulles watched these specialists intently, and at the first sign of what he suspected to be a possible threat to the tight and straight line-of-command between himself and the President, he straightened out the difficulty quickly. . . . In every instance where Dulles decided the situation was intolerable, he insisted on a change, and the President without exception went along with his wishes.

Characteristically, Sherman Adams reports, Dulles said to him suspiciously one day that Rockefeller seemed to be building up a big staff: 'He's got them down at Quantico and nobody knows what they're doing.' Again, Dulles 'wanted tight control over the formulation of [foreign aid] policy but this was difficult, particularly with a man of Stassen's dynamic disposition running the operations. So he persuaded the President to move the agency back into the State Department.' Disposing of Nelson Rockefeller's proposal for a presidential assistant in foreign affairs, he insisted that 'nothing should come between the Secretary of State and the President.'[8]

Even when Dulles was physically laid low, in the central period of the 1956 crisis, Eisenhower deferred to his known views, as conveyed by his lieutenants, especially Herbert Hoover. 'The President passed along to the State Department Eden's proposal for a personal visit to Washington with his own view that it would be good for the world . . . the consensus of opinion was that the visit was premature and should be discouraged.'[9] Christian Herter, who succeeded Dulles as Secretary of State for what may be regarded as the long 'lame-duck' period of the Republican administration, 1959 and 1960, was a much-liked man in England as elsewhere, and his relations with Selwyn Lloyd and Macmillan are reported to have been cordial. But undoubtedly, looking back over the eight years of the Republican administration as a whole, the one personality which emerges as clear, forceful, formidable, certain of itself and of where the West should go, was that of Dulles. And almost alone of major recent American policy-makers, Dulles found his international friendships, such as they were, on the Continent, not in Britain. His only close personal relations were with Jean Monnet and with Adenauer: even his post-graduate university experience had been at the Sorbonne, whereas Oxford was almost as pervasive as Harvard in the personal backgrounds of the men around Kennedy.

However, it was not merely the influence of Dulles, that respectable and disastrous personage, that marks the decisive difference in individual attitudes in the Eisen-

---

[8] Adams, pp. 88–91, 460.
[9] See R. Drummond and G. Coblentz, *Duel at the Brink* (1960).

hower and Kennedy administrations. There are two main intellectual traditions, or contexts of thought, in both American and British foreign-policy making. Since they are subtly different, though related, I will call them nationalist and reformist in America, traditionalist and dissentient in Britain. The differences in both countries relate to attitudes to the use and cultivation of power. Easiness of intellectual relations between foreign-policy makers in England and America depends a good deal on how well matched their respective blends of the two traditions are at any particular time. And though Dulles and his immediate advisers were not nearly as much in the reformist or Wilsonian stream of thought as people assumed from Dulles's fondness for moral platitudes, nevertheless the advent of the Kennedy administration represented a sharp shift away from any tendencies of this sort. Indeed, if one takes some of Kennedy's advisers as representing the present phase of the nationalist tradition in American thought on foreign policy, one can say that it has come so close to the traditionalist strand in Britain, in the use of such concepts as the balance of power, as to be almost indistinguishable from it.[10] Only Chester Bowles, among major administration figures, could perhaps be assigned to the reformist stream of thought, and he, appropriately, was assigned by Kennedy to India, where it still strikes a responsive intellectual chord. If there is any intellectual incompatibility between the climates of opinion in which foreign policy is made in London and Washington at present, it arises from dissentient

[10] A book by W. W. Rostow, Kennedy's Chief of the Policy Planning Division of the State Department, *The United States in the World Arena* (1961) offers a comprehensive set of intellectual attitudes among policy-formulators. The writings of Hans Morgenthau, C. B. Marshall, Paul Nitze, Roger Hilsman, Arthur Schlesinger, Theodore White also offer useful guidelines to the general intellectual context on which policy is made. No comparable list can be provided for the Republican administration, which was a good deal less articulate on paper.

opinion having more impact on decision-makers in London than reformist opinion has on their counterparts in Washington, except on some quasi-colonial issues.

The last months of the Eisenhower administration in 1960 coincided with the end of any very serious striving after a fully independent British nuclear strike-force. In 1960 four Russian military rockets were fired about 8,000 miles and apparently attained an accuracy of 2–3 miles at target. The effect of this demonstration of rocket guidance was to downgrade the usefulness of all fixed-site military missiles under development, including, most importantly, the Blue Streak rocket, Britain's only promising bid for an independent-delivery vehicle to carry her nuclear weapons in the post-bomber era. Blue Streak was due to operate from a fixed site, and in a world of four-minute warnings was not regarded as likely to be effective enough to warrant further development. Its cancellation in April 1960 was followed two months later by the announcement that Britain would buy Skybolt, then regarded as likely to extend the life of the manned bomber over the late 1960s and early 1970s, and adaptable to the later models of the V-bomber. It is remarkable that this announcement, the true closing of the period when Britain could be said to be making an effort to construct a deterrent force on a substantial do-it-yourself basis,[11] should have caused much less stir than the later cancellation of Skybolt, when the change was only from dependence on one form of American missile to dependence on another and really more suitable one.

Both sides of British politics had in fact moved closer to

[11] There did remain a British weapon regarded as viable for the transition period, (the quasi-obsolescence of the long-range bomber in the late 1960s) in the air-borne stand-off bomb, Blue Steel. This could conceivably have been developed to extend its range from the present 200 miles, but the rewards of doing so were judged not worth the effort, since it could hardly have affected the situation after about 1970.

defensive dependence on America by late 1961. In 1960, more than in any year since 1950, there had seemed a danger that the alternative government for Britain, the Labour Party, might find itself committed to a line in defence and foreign policy which could potentially lead it out of the American camp into the neutralist wilderness (or garden, according to choice). This was the year of peak impact of the CND, the movement of revolt against nuclear weapons, which had risen from feeble beginnings in 1957 to such a degree of influence within the Labour Party as to enable it at Scarborough in September 1960 to secure the adoption of a resolution calling for the uni-lateral renunciation of nuclear weapons. It is true that for Britain to renounce her own nuclear strike force would not greatly have furrowed many American brows either in 1960 or later. Both Republican and Democratic admini-strations have been conscious of the advantages from the point of view of the two dominant powers of the reserva-tion to themselves of the nuclear oligopoly. But the emo-tional overtone of the Scarborough resolution was hope not only for the giving up of the British weapons (essen-tially an issue of account only for Britain's own diplomatic leverage) but of British exit from nuclear alliances, which would imply the British abandonment of NATO and pre-sumably any other arrangements essentially dependent on American power. This would have meant a real reshuffle of diplomatic alignments, the most important *political* swing of the balance against America since 1949. There-fore Gaitskell's declaration, as the potential alternative Prime Minister at Scarborough, that he would 'fight and fight and fight again' to reverse the conference decision, and his actual success in getting it reversed at the follow-ing year's conference, at Blackpool in October 1961, was of great moment. It was Gaitskell's success in getting his party to look at the question of British nuclear weapons,

not in the context of an anti-American neutralism but in
the context of a further integration of NATO and a more
complete dependence on the U.S., that made it possible
for his successor, Harold Wilson, to advance lines of
Labour Party policy on defence and foreign affairs that
appeared in some (not all) respects more palatable to the
American administration than those of the Conservative
government. Macmillan's decision to seek full membership
of EEC for Britain was of course much more in line with
American policy than the Labour Party's doubts. All in
all, in late 1961, as 'the Kennedy changes' began to
go into effect, the government and even the potential
alternative government in Britain had less reason to
expect dissension with America than in many previous
years.

The same was not true of France. Where the British
government had in effect settled for influence with Washington, General de Gaulle remained preoccupied with
independence. Again, this contrast in attitudes is not surprising. Over the past twenty-two years British policy-
makers have won enough of their arguments with Washington to make reasonable the conviction that the cultivat-
ing of this relationship is their most useful line of diplomatic action. France, and de Gaulle personally, have had
a much lower percentage of successes. Looking back, one
is struck by the number of grudges which any French
nationalist might feel against 'the Anglo-Saxons'. This
feeling emerges at surprising times and places, as when
François Mauriac, in November 1960, commented on
Kennedy's election with the remark that 'in 1944 the
Americans coldly pulverized [French] villages and
churches although they could have avoided doing so' and
went on to reflect: 'Make no mistake, the day he [Ken-
nedy] considered it necessary to strike [against French
interests] he would strike. . . . But that will not happen so

long as two stars shine on the uniform of Charles de Gaulle.'[12]

The peak period of French resentment and irritation at the policies of its American ally was probably in 1953-6. In 1953-4 the chief source was anger at Dulles's rather tactless effort to pressure France into the EDC treaty, especially his famous threat of an 'agonizing reappraisal' of American alliances if the treaty were rejected. It was said in Paris that some of the Deputies who voted to drop the EDC project in August 1954 did so as much in protest against Dulles as in protest against the treaty itself. From then into early 1955 there was also the issue of American policy in Indo-China. On this question America managed to irk both the left and the right wing of French opinion. The left was angered by the early period of American intervention, in 1953-4, and played much on the allegation that this was a case of America fighting the cold war in Asia to the last Frenchman. There was an ill-tempered Paris joke that France need not worry about the dollar gap because she had one export that undersold all others: blood for Indo-China. On the other hand the outcome of events in late 1954 and early 1955 embittered the right. Many Frenchmen at the time were inclined to see America as a far more dangerous enemy to residual French interests than Ho Chi Minh. It was, after all, the Americans who insisted on sustaining Ngo Dinh Diem, a strongly anti-French nationalist, as Prime Minister, who backed him against the various French efforts to overturn him in 1955-6, and who insisted on paying dollar aid direct to the nationalist government, thus securing its survival. That France saved so little from the post-Dien-Bien-Phu wreckage of her empire in Indo-China was felt among the French right to be far more attributable to the Americans than to the Communists, as perhaps it was. In fact in the

[12] Quoted by Roy Alan, 'Algeria', *New Leader*, 5 Mar. 1962.

whole sphere of colonial policy the French have a long list of grievances against 'the Anglo-Saxons', from the memory of Roosevelt's encouragement of the Sultan of Morocco during the Casablanca Conference, and his famous remark about the French having milked the Indo-Chinese cow long enough, to the Anglo-American pressure against any restoration of French influence in Syria and the Lebanon during the war and just afterwards, their less than sympathetic attitude in the French conflicts with the Moroccan and Tunisian nationalists and in France's struggle in Algeria, as demonstrated for instance in their continuing supply of arms to Tunisia despite a high probability that these arms would ultimately reach the Algerian nationalists. Even on the one occasion in which France found Britain an apparently useful ally in her dealings with the Arabs, Suez, Britain turned out from the French view to be a broken reed, collapsing under the pressure of American disapproval. There was no significant domestic political opposition in France to the Suez invasion, so the forced abandonment of the enterprise was just another case, from the French standpoint, of France being again a victim of the infirmity of purpose or the downright perfidy of 'the Anglo-Saxons'. Aside from these national scores, de Gaulle had a few of his own, especially against the Americans, dating from the wartime conflicts with Roosevelt and Cordell Hull. The whole issue of continued American recognition of the Vichy government, and the Darlan imbroglio in North Africa, were personal slaps in the face for him. And it must be remembered that this American policy was administered by Eisenhower himself, with Macmillan, then a junior member of Churchill's government, as his political adviser (though to Macmillan's credit it must be said that he was arguing for de Gaulle at this time). Finally, there was the episode in 1958, still somewhat obscure, in which de Gaulle suggested the establishment of a three-power directorate, including France, for NATO, and was politely rebuffed by Eisenhower. Thus again one may say that there is a contrast between Britain and France in the apparent lessons to be drawn from recent historical experience. Whereas the British looking back to 1940, were necessarily struck by the importance of the American connexion to Britain's survival and power, the present French leadership, looking back over the same period, was more likely to be struck by a consciousness that French national interests had not been over tenderly treated by her 'Anglo-Saxon' allies, and that France might do better if she could acquire (whether by nuclear weapons or the leadership of Europe) rather more ability to exert an independent diplomatic leverage.

And de Gaulle, as has been said, had come to power just at the moment at which Europe as a whole received a sudden accretion of diplomatic leverage through a shift in the world balance of power. The success of the Russians in putting up the first sputnik, or rather what that success indicated about the *technological* balance of the foreseeable future, transformed NATO from an American security guarantee to Europe into an organization equally vital to America's own defence, a true mutual-defensive society with the balance of dependence almost even on the two sides of the Atlantic. In thus raising the importance of the organization for America's *own* security (as against that of the European powers), this change in the technological balance made the European members of NATO more important as allies to America, and thus raised their diplomatic leverage *vis-à-vis* America. Moreover the simple facts of geography give France an almost invincible position of advantage *vis-à-vis* her NATO allies. The whole of NATO's conventional strategy in Europe depends on France as a fulcrum. NATO's supply routes and 'infrastructure' must lie in France. De Gaulle was thus in fact the inheritor of a situation in which the prospects for the pursuit of enhanced diplomatic status for France were more promising than they had been since 1940. The strategic changes put into effect by Kennedy and Mc-Namara enhanced this French diplomatic leverage. For the conventional, or even the tactical-atomic defence of Europe (as against deterrence by the threat of strategic nuclear strike) are hardly conceivable without French co-operation. And France's interests here pointed in a very similar direction to Germany's.

For ten years after West Germany's re-emergence as a diplomatic entity in 1949, the unquestioned first principle of Dr Adenauer's foreign policy had been that there was no substitute for the American alliance as far as German security was concerned, and that there was no alternative backing to America's in the claims West Germany eventually had to make on Russia, claims in the first instance about the restoration of free choice in East Germany, and in the second instance about the restoration of the lost territories. 'Negotiation from strength' as a Western policy had a more concrete meaning for Dr Adenauer than for any of the other Western leaders. It meant that the diplomatic leverage of the Western alliance was the only 'situation of strength' from which negotiations could safely be entered with Russia for the reunification of Germany and the regaining of the lost territories. Thus the reunification of Germany had to wait on the integration of the West, and there followed logically the rejection of such otherwise-attractive-seeming gambits as the Soviet note of March 1952 offering, apparently, reunification in exchange for neutrality, with some faint prospect of the reunification being conducted on the basis of acceptable electoral arrangements. In a sense this was *necessarily* the policy of the German government in the period to 1958, because there was no other policy domestically and internationally feasible. (The often-paraded spectre of the 'new Rapallo' is really no more than a spectre in this period: it is not a feasible alternative policy, since both power considerations and domestic politics ruled it out. The Russia of the original Rapallo was a militarily prostrate state, beaten and forced to the harshest treaty of modern times [Brest-Litovsk] by the German army only four years earlier, then beaten again by Poland and racked by civil war. And moreover it was held off from Germany by a 'cordon sanitaire' of weaker states, and was diplomatically quite isolated. To assume that because Germany could make a useful deal with that Russia in 1922, it could as well do so with the Russia of 1962, is to assume that a man who was prepared to play pat-a-cake with a new-born tiger kitten will be prepared to do the same with a full-grown and conspicuously sabre-toothed tiger. At any rate, the prosperous, Catholic, conservative bourgeoisie who were the dominant political group in Dr Adenauer's Germany were not the people for such adventures.)

Thus in this period there was no possibility of conflict, as far as Germany was concerned, between 'Europe' and the Atlantic alliance. For Germany, as for France, the question of getting on with the old European enemy revolved round the fact of its having acquired the new character of a fellow-member of the American-alliance system. Dr Adenauer's relations with Dulles were far warmer and closer than his relations with any of the leaders of the Fourth Republic, or any of the British postwar leaders, and America was West Germany's sponsor (against the doubts of Britain and, at that time, of France) in the whole question of its entry to the Atlantic alliance. Only after the initiation of the second Berlin crisis by Khrushchev in November 1958 did any consciousness become visible in Bonn or Washington of how far American and German estimates of the Western interest in Central

Europe might possibly diverge. The potential divergence was not on the question of Berlin itself, where America remained fully committed to the retention of a Western presence, but on the question of dealings with the East German authorities. Even while Dulles was in control of policy, Washington would not back Adenauer's insistence on a stony refusal to have anything to do with the East Germans, even as agents of the Russians. After Dulles's death, and still more after the advent of the Democrats to power, American-German official relations lost what personal warmth they had earlier had. (Kennedy's visit to Germany in 1963, while a tremendous success at the public level, was reported to have been considerably less than that at the level of his personal relations with *der Alte*.) Dr Adenauer could hardly be expected to take kindly to seeing the overall political and strategic command of the alliance to which he has pinned Germany's diplomatic hopes fall under the command of a man almost of his grandchildren's generation. Not that it was altogether a matter of generations: Kennedy's defeat of Nixon for the White House meant the subjecting of the familiar policies of the Dulles period to new scrutinies by new men, and meant that new solutions might be sought on questions such as the security of Berlin. Dr Adenauer did not like any of Kennedy's new approaches to the Russians, especially not the notion of an international authority on which the East Germans would be represented. It seems to have been with protests on this issue that the West German ambassador in Washington, Herr Grewe, made himself so unpopular in the State Department (or perhaps in the White House itself) that he had to be recalled as, in effect, *persona non grata*. Doubtless incidents of this sort are too obscure and too muffled in diplomatic language to have much effect beyond policy-making circles, but there have been a few indications that Germany's attachment to the

American alliance was coming under some strain at the level of the man in the street, especially the man in the Berlin street. An uncomfortably symbolic air brooded over the case of the young East German, Peter Fechter, who had to be allowed to bleed to death, just the other side of the Wall and in full view of his countrymen, because the American troops had orders not to risk an incident with the Russians. It was strongly enough felt to produce some anti-American demonstrations by West Berliners, then and on the second anniversary of the Wall.

Kennedy was unavoidably caught on the East German issue, between America's interests as leader of a *world* coalition, and the specific interests of his German ally. As the leader of a world coalition he had to be concerned to keep the level of tension with Russia in Central Europe relatively low, not only in the general cause of peace but in the urgent immediate interest of being able to devote time, attention, and resources to 'mending fences' elsewhere on the world front, particularly in Latin America and in South Asia, where such fences as exist were already disappearing in the undergrowth. Therefore he had to seek some *modus vivendi* with Russia in Central Europe. But even the coldest *modus vivendi* entails some degree of recognition (not formal recognition, of course) of East Germany, and this must infringe West Germany's diplomatic interest in maintaining its status as the sole government recognized as 'legitimate' in Germany, the sole authentic spokesman for the German people. This status is very important to West Germany: it is one of the chief benefits deriving from the 1954 agreements that regulated German entry to NATO. Dr Adenauer's successors must measure Germany's place in the Western-alliance structure primarily by Germany's need for security against Russia and the importance of the American connexion in this respect. But they must also ask (if only because of domestic pressures) how helpful this alliance structure is in negotiating their own diplomatic objectives *vis-à-vis* Russia. And it can hardly be denied that the prospects in this respect look no more promising now than they did when Dr Adenauer established his line of policy in 1949–50.

Up to 1958, even if the Germans found the Atlantic Community not meeting all their national diplomatic hopes, there was nothing much they could do about it, since there was no place else to go. But from that time there has been potentially Carolingian Europe, possibly with several advantages as a niche from which to negotiate with the Americans, if not the Russians. One may note the complementarity of German and French interests on this matter. An effective Carolingian Europe must undoubtedly be a nuclear-armed Europe, if one is equating 'effectiveness' with ability to deal on anything approaching equal terms with the other nuclear powers. And on this issue American preoccupations cut as sharply across French ones as they do across German ones on the question of the *status quo* in East Germany, and for much the same reason. Avoiding the diffusion of nuclear forces, and maintaining her own quasi-monopoly of decision in this field, are just as important for America as elements of a potential tension-lowering accommodation with Russia as is an agreed *modus vivendi* in Central Europe. It must thus be stressed that the potential divergences of interest between America on the one hand and France and Germany on the other were *not* simply aspects of the personalities of Adenauer and de Gaulle. No doubt Adenauer's insistence on access routes to Berlin and de Gaulle's pursuit of enhanced status for France owed much to personal factors, but there are real asymmetries of national interest involved, which will not vanish even when both veterans have quitted the scene, and which are likely to become more and more distinct by the very process of growth of European strength and military potential. (There are also conflicts of interest within the French-German alliance, notably over German reunification, which may operate ultimately to inhibit its development, but which for the time being are kept strategically suppressed.)

President Kennedy was much more willing than the Europeans themselves not only to assume a persistence of the Atlantic orientation of Europe, but to envisage a leap from that to an integrated 'Atlantic partnership'. His Independence Day speech on 6 July 1962 was a very striking exemplification of his boldness of mind in this respect. He used even the phrases of the original Declaration of Independence to speak up for the concept of interdependence. Yet it is not by any means certain that Europe would feel any necessary enthusiasm for such a prospect. To the questions: would it necessarily conduce to Europe's security? to its prosperity? to its ability to end the cleavage down its own centre? the answers must at best be uncertain. The American administration, not at all unreasonably, sees Atlantic partnership as a means towards a more equal sharing of burdens, of which at present America bears the heavy end, not only in military costs in NATO but in aid costs for the underdeveloped world. But this aspect of 'partnership' is not likely to rouse enthusiasm in Europe. Nor could the submerging of Europe in the general Atlantic Community be agreeable to those newly and pridefully conscious of the European identity and with an itch to see the new Europe as *tertius gaudens* in the world's game.

The meaning of Nassau

When one views the issue in this light, it comes to seem almost inevitable that the event which precipitated General de Gaulle's decision to break off the negotiations for British entry into the Common Market should have been Macmillan's acceptance, at the Nassau meeting with President Kennedy, of Polaris instead of Skybolt as the future equipment of the British nuclear force. The meaning of this decision was the growing *integration* of British nuclear power with American, rather than a growing *independence* of a joint European nuclear force supplied by France and Britain. That is to say, it was an indication of the persistent British adhesion to the Atlantic rather than the Carolingian view of Europe's future, and it was clearly this portentous issue, rather than any remaining difficulties about agriculture or the Commonwealth, which led de Gaulle to conclude, as he said, that Britain was not yet ready to enter Europe, and led Macmillan to reproach de Gaulle, later, with believing that Europe 'can live alone, without friends and without allies'. This strategic cleavage after Nassau, and Britain's situation on the American rather than the Continental side of the dichotomy, had begun to be indicated several months before the break, and more especially after McNamara's well-known speech about independent deterrents in June 1962. To understand the nature of the issues involved one must look rather more closely at the strategic stance which the Kennedy administration had reached by this point in its tenure of office.

Here the analysis must depend heavily on the American academic strategists with access to administration thinking, on Professor Henry Kissinger,[13] for instance, though there are some variations in accounts given by other experts in the field on the finer points of strategic-diplomatic doctrine. A central preoccupation of the President's advisers is the problem of retaining in American hands the

---

[13] See his 'Nato's Nuclear Dilemma', *The Reporter*, 28 Mar. 1963, pp. 22–33; also Michael Brower, 'Nuclear Strategy of the Kennedy Administration', *Bull. of Atomic Scientists*, Oct. 1962, and Alastair Buchan, 'Nassau Reconsidered' *New Republic*, 2 Mar. 1963.

ability 'to conduct "centrally controlled" nuclear war which provides the opponent a maximum incentive to spare the civilian population by giving us the option to do likewise[14] (the 'no-cities' doctrine). This entails that the strategic nuclear weapons of the alliance must be integrated and responsive to a single chain of command: in other words, any non-American element must be an adjunct to the U.S. strategic forces. The notion of tactical nuclear weapons has come to be regarded with disfavour and scepticism, in that they are not easily susceptible to central control and entail a risk of escalation. Thus since the American strategists considered 'European national nuclear forces irrelevant and tactical nuclear weapons over-valued',[15] it followed that the European contribution to NATO should be in conventional forces, and that there should be a 'conventional' capability to deal with even 'a massive, sustained Soviet offensive'. This represents a reversal, made explicit in the Nassau communiqué, of the earlier Western strategic doctrine which had represented conventional and nuclear forces as, respectively, the 'shield and sword' of NATO: that is, nuclear strike had been the real Western military sanction against Russia, conventional forces merely a protective device to impose, at best, what was called 'a pause' (expected duration never defined) in the incursion of Soviet troops while either nuclear power or diplomatic arrangement (or a blend) effected the settlement. In the new doctrine nuclear power becomes merely the shield: conventional forces have the far more exacting role of providing the major military sanction against conventional aggression in Europe.

This doctrine does not imply a down-grading in size in American nuclear forces: quite the contrary, since the striking power needed for the new concept of their role is,

[14] Kissinger, in *The Reporter*, 28 Mar. 1963.
[15] Ibid.

G

curiously enough, much greater than that implied in the old doctrine of 'massive retaliation'. According to Mc-Namara, U.S. capability should be great enough to absorb a Soviet [pre-emptive?] blow, and then

to strike back first at the Soviet bomber bases, missile sites, and other military installations associated with their long-range nuclear forces to reduce the power of any follow-on attack—and then, if necessary, strike back at the Soviet urban and industrial complex in a controlled and deliberate way.[16]

The U.S. nuclear forces required by such a strategic doctrine would necessarily be much larger than the Soviet nuclear-strike forces they faced. By the American accounting, they were in fact three or four times the size of the equivalent Soviet forces as at the time of the test-ban treaty. But, as Kissinger points out, a war of attrition cannot be to the interest of the weaker side, and so the logical Soviet nuclear strategy would be to reject this doctrine and to respond by the threat or actuality of destroying cities, perhaps (to use the standard euphemism) in a 'controlled' way. The crux of the question is: which cities? And here it cannot be denied that both from the point of view of feasibility (since they can far more readily be hit) and from the point of view of what one might call prudential Soviet calculations about American responses, the obvious answer would seem to be 'European cities'. To use Kissinger's understatement: 'In these conditions, the prospect of "controlling" general war cannot be an incentive to the Europeans to give up their own nuclear programs; the contrary is likely to be the case.'[17] And he goes on:

If the NATO area is looked on as a unit, a strategy that exposes a limited territory to the fluctuations of conventional

[16] Statement of Jan. 1963, cited ibid., p. 25.
[17] Ibid.

combat may seem eminently sensible. To the allies on whose
territory such a war would be fought, however, a Soviet
penetration of even a hundred miles may well spell the end of
their national existence. They have a compelling incentive to
strive for a strategy that poses the threat of maximum devastation for the Soviets. Europeans are almost inevitably more
concerned with deterrence than with defense. They will prefer
a strategy that seeks to magnify the risks of the aggressor rather
than reduce the losses of the defender.[18]

If Britain were in precisely the same degree of danger as
West Germany from Soviet conventional forces, or if her
nuclear strike-forces were viewed, by the American leadership, in quite the same way as France's, then no doubt
Britain would belong on the Continental rather than the
American side of the strategic dichotomy. But neither of
these things is in fact true: Britain remains an island, and
in some ways the nuclear age has put the prospect of conventional sea-borne invasion against a power with even a
minor degree of atomic strike rather more firmly out of
court than it was in the second world war. So that with
respect to conventional warfare the historic difference between Britain and the Continental powers is maintained.
and as to the question of 'nuclear autonomy' *vis-à-vis*
America, the British power of nuclear strike, though often
referred to as an 'independent deterrent', has in fact since
1960 been called in official circles 'an independent contribution to the Western deterrent', a phrase whose degree
of ambiguity nicely accords with the reality of the situation. As this essay has hoped to show, the element of
'reinsurance' or autonomy in the British attitude towards
America in the advanced-weapons field has always been
very much offset by a purposive acceptance of integration
and a willingness since 1960 to acquiesce in considerable
real dependence, provided it was not so blatant as to

[18] Ibid., p 27.

undermine Britain's diplomatic standing among the powers.

It is tempting to maintain that the nuclear fig-leaf of apparent independence that Britain has clung to is related less to the diplomatic *milieux* in which Britain deals with the powers, than to the hustings from which the government must deal with the electorate. Tempting but unfair, for in fact the garments of the repentant sinner which it could assume, once it had given up nuclear weapons, would probably serve quite well with the electorate: it is only in the diplomatic counting-houses that they would appear as little convincing as the Emperor's new clothes. In reality, quite apart from any advantages it may or may not have conferred on the government *vis-à-vis* the electorate, one could readily construct an argument to show that on the whole, over the entire period 1945–63, the sums expended on the advanced-weapons system had certainly not proved what in America might be called 'a less good buy, defence-wise' than the conventional forces. Over the whole period their construction and maintenance has absorbed about 10 per cent of each year's defence expenditure. And in times of peace or cold war, what military establishments may be presumed to buy is diplomatic leverage. So to prove that the creation of this force was a bad decision in terms of defence economics one would have to show that it was less than one-ninth as effective in promoting Britain's general diplomatic objectives as the remainder of the military establishment, the whole of the conventional forces. The most serious direct use made of the British conventional forces to secure a national objective during this period was, of course, Suez, which can hardly be regarded as a glowing testimonial to their usefulness. Diplomatically, it is true, the 'alliance' use of them, in the sense of the commitment of four divisions to NATO, was what clinched the WEU arrangement on which NATO's land forces in Europe depended. But though the conventional forces certainly bought some diplomatic leverage in this matter and in relation to minor powers, the total remains unimpressive. If one endeavours to relate the military establishment that a country decides to buy to the particular powers in relation to which it desires to purchase diplomatic standing or leverage, one must maintain that the rational choice in Britain's case was to purchase these commodities *vis-à-vis* America and Russia, since Britain's national interests are much more bound up with the central balance between these two powers than with any local balance, *including that in Europe*. And it is uncommonly difficult to see precisely in what way the decision to spend the £200 million a year that was in fact spent on the strike-forces on conventional forces instead, would have improved her diplomatic leverage with respect to either America or Russia.[19] It is no argument to say that both American administrations would have preferred to see more British land forces in BAOR. We are considering how to maximize influence, not how to be a model ally. Who would be prepared to maintain that totally biddable persons exert more influence on the decisions of others than occasionally intransigent ones? Even with respect to entry into Europe, the nuclear strike-force was in fact a more important diplomatic card, *if the Prime Minister had chosen to play it*, than the conventional forces. It is no secret that de Gaulle was strongly interested in British co-operation in the building of the French

[19] Patrick Gordon-Walker, talking of Labour's intentions with regard to the funds saved from the strike-force, has admitted that his prospective government does not even believe that they can be used to increase the conventional forces, but merely to improve their equipment. This surely is a *reductio ad absurdum* of the 'conventional-forces-are-more-diplomatically-useful' argument. One might maintain that larger conventional forces mean more diplomatic leverage, but surely not that better mortars for BAOR more than compensate for the ending of a force whose strike power is far greater than that of all the conventional forces on the central front put together.

strike-force. After all, Britain has had almost ten years'
advantage over France in the production of fissile material,
and the use of British installations which are at present
running in low gear, since the build-up of weapon stocks
has been more than adequate to the means of delivery,
would have greatly eased the strain on French resources
represented by such projects as the building of the plant
at Pierrelatte. British co-operation would have been still
more valuable with regard to means of delivery, either of
rockets or nuclear submarines, after the first-era French
vehicle, the Mirage IV, becomes obsolescent. (Some
American comment has insisted that in view of the Russian
development of air defences it must be regarded as obsolescent even as it goes into service.) The strength of French
feeling as to the usefulness of British co-operation in this
field is indicated by the reported remark of a French
defence official, after Nassau, that Britain's agreement was
'incompatible with choosing Europe'. The Skybolt cancellation itself had, of course, confirmed the French view
that the dependence of Europe on American weaponry
was not to be tolerated, since American undertakings
were unreliable. But to have used British nuclear power
for leverage in this particular diplomatic context would
have been incompatible with the whole notion of the
Anglo-American relation as the closest of Britain's diplomatic ties, and specifically might have meant the probable
loss (though this is uncertain) of the post-1958 mitigation
of the McMahon Act in Britain's favour.

The diplomatic leverage conferred by nuclear weapons
was even more clearly indicated a few months later in an
area infinitely more vital to Britain, the central balance.
On what basis, if not that of her own possession of nuclear
weapons, was Britain a member of the three-power talks
which concluded the test-ban treaty? Some comment has
spoken as if British entry to these talks might be attributed

to the Commonwealth,[20] or to Macmillan's personal wisdom, or something of the sort. But this line of argument can be demolished with a single question. Conceivably these considerations could be held to be important if America alone chose the participants, but even if they could be an adequate entry fee *vis-à-vis* Kennedy, *what then would be the entry fee vis-à-vis Khrushchev*? Is it really to be conceived that he would choose to face two Western interlocuteurs rather than one, if one of them had no independent standing? Especially in view of the questions this would raise from China? Even the technical contributions by British scientists, which were highly significant in the preliminary stages of the discussions, were dependent on access to research work only made possible by this independent standing. And the diplomatic endeavours to push the treaty, both at the level of the Foreign Office negotiators and at the level of the Prime Minister likewise depended on this *locus standi*. How do you argue a case if you have not the entry card which alone admits to the room where the argument is being conducted? Membership of these talks was of importance not only for the test-ban treaty itself, but for entry to the process in which it marks an early but crucially important stage, the developing process of joint management by the nuclear oligarchs of the central balance of power.

However, to revert for a moment to the question of Britain's diplomatic bargaining power within the Anglo-American alliance, or the Western alliance as a whole, one must observe that this is a field in which the realities are

[20] Though in fact the American administration's view of the Commonwealth was rather that expressed by Acheson in his West Point speech: that it is an organization 'which has no political structure, or unity, or strength, and enjoys a fragile and precarious economic relationship by means of the sterling area and preferences in the British market'. Since British liberal opinion in recent years has consistently propounded the view that the Commonwealth, however sentimentally desirable, is quite irrelevant in power relations, it cannot logically expect the Americans to take the opposite view.

often obscured by the sentimental pretence that a total harmony of interests is the norm for relationships between allies. In reality diplomatic bargaining, conflicts of will and interest and their adjustment, are hardly less the staple fact of life between allies than between enemies. What determines whose will prevails when there is difference of opinion, or even sharp conflict? The answer must be essentially power, with influence as one of its variants. One might say that in diplomacy, as in economic life, any entity—in this case the state—has an aspect in which it is a 'consumer' and an aspect in which it is a 'producer' of security. If it were not in some way a consumer of security in relation to the alliance—that is, if the alliance could add nothing to its security—there would be no reason, other than altruism, for its being a member. Contrariwise, if it were not in some aspect a producer of security—that is, if it could add nothing to the general strength of the alliance —the other members would have no reason, other than altruism, for letting it be a member. And since altruism is not a very powerful motive in international politics, one may regard a state's membership of an alliance as providing a *prima facie* case for supposing that it has functions both as producer and consumer of security in relation to that alliance as a whole. Its leverage *vis-à-vis* the other members of the alliance will depend on the relation between its needs as a consumer and its potentialities as a producer of security, its credit or debit balance in the security bank. If one were arranging the members of the American alliance structure along a scale, they would all come out net debtors *vis-à-vis* America, in the sense that the alliance with America adds more to the security of each than alliance with the other power concerned adds to the security of America. But the power closest to the 'net creditor' end of the scale would be Britain, with only France as a close rival. There are a number of factors in-

volved in this accounting for each of the powers concerned: the 'alternative options' available, the degree to
which the country concerned is vulnerable to the most
probable threats, and the extent of its quarrels with the
potential adversary are all factors in determining its place
on the producer-consumer scale, as well as its own intrinsic military strength. For instance Germany, which on the
basis of a simple division-count in conventional strength
might seem to belong with Britain and France close to the
'net producer' end of the scale, may be seen, when these
diplomatic factors are taken into consideration, to belong
with, say, Denmark and Turkey at the other end of the
scale, as the most vulnerable of the major powers. But
though intrinsic military strength is not the sole deter-
minant of one's place in the security scale, it must be of
major importance, especially when it happens to be nuclear
strength. The French argument that twenty nuclear
weapons at the disposal of the French government consti-
tute a more effective deterrent force, as far as *French*
interests are concerned, than 2,000 nuclear bombs at the
disposal of an ally of France, *who has his own interests to
think of*, has been much derided for its apparent over-
simplifications and its inherent scepticism about the American commitment to Europe. Yet the calculation that must
be made is not about the present President's intentions or
even about the intentions of his successors: it is about what
the *Russians* may calculate at some future date, as to
American intentions. And Russian calculations concerning
American intent and resolution have not always been dis-
tinguished by sagacity, as witness the original decision to
put missiles into Cuba. One must hope that Khrushchev's
successors as well as Khrushchev himself will prove to have
learned from this episode to respect the basic toughness of
America's determination to preserve her own sphere of
power. But a built-in bias towards error is predictable in

Russian calculation in this field, because of their constant doctrinal expectation of rifts in the capitalist camp, and their unshakeable belief that they themselves represent the wave of the future, whose adversaries must necessarily at some point crumple and fall apart. Therefore the enigma of the future is Russian calculations about American (or other Western) *will*, not about American *capabilities*. And who, reading diplomatic history, could fail to note that the great powers' propensity to defend their allies' interests has been somewhat less pronounced than their propensity to defend their own?

The strategic dichotomy

In any case, whatever one's judgement of the diplomatic expediency (or, of course, the morality) of the British decisions of 1947–62 that created the nuclear strike-force, it was indubitably a fact that by the time at which serious discussion of the central power-balance began to be undertaken, early in 1963, these decisions had resulted in her strategic situation being closer to that of the nuclear oligarchs than to that of the other European powers. This was particularly the case with regard to strategic choices, and especially the 'no-cities' doctrine. Presumably it is not necessary to underline the importance as a question in the simplest and most absolute sense of the survival of the national community for Britain to be able to influence the choices of both dominant powers when it comes to 'targeting'. This was the military (as against the diplomatic) justification of the notion of an independent deterrent back in 1957, and it cannot have done other than increase in importance now that the central strategic argument has moved into the rarified air of 'selective response' and 'city-bargaining'. The degree of independent nuclear power needed to modify (if things should come to so desperate a pass) Russian target choices *vis-à-vis* Britain does not have to be anything like that of the dominant powers. It merely has to be that of effectively threatening reprisals to avert the worst possibilities. A system of joint-targeting was put into effect between Britain and America in 1958 because of the growth of the British nuclear strike-force: it represents one of the least-considered but most vital elements in the strategic relation.

The effect of the Nassau decision, that is the substitution of Polaris for Skybolt, changed the future nature of the British strike-force but not its potential ability to influence Russian strategic choices. In respect of the long-term viability of British power in this field it is clear that the substitution was one devoutly to be wished. If a country as large as the U.S. nevertheless chooses to put its final-resort deterrent to sea, the incentive for one as small as Britain to do so must be much greater. Nuclear submarines hiding at sea may not be totally invulnerable, but they are a great deal less vulnerable, according to expert opinion, than any other available vehicle of nuclear power. This is strikingly illustrated by the recent testimony of McNamara himself. Giving evidence to the House Armed Services Committee in January 1963 he said that American counter-force strength was designed to destroy virtually all of the soft and semi-hard military targets in the Soviet Union and a proportion of the hardened sites. *But no significant capacity for destroying missile-carrying submarines would be developed.* If the American administration is prepared to acquiesce in the view that it cannot, for the foreseeable future, expect to develop a significant capacity for destroying Soviet missile-carrying submarines, then the technological difficulties in this field, as seen by the people who know the technology best, must indeed be formidable. And what applies to the Soviet submarines applies with more force to the American and prospective British ones, since the Soviet fleet is mostly short-range and surface-firing. Besides, Polaris submarines have, as against missiles and aircraft, the enormous advantage (despite the Holy Loch demonstrators) of not attracting nuclear strike to the home territory, since in periods of tension they can and would be kept at sea for weeks at a time, and there would be no point for the enemy in wasting nuclear-strike power on empty bases. In terms of the evolution of delivery vehicles, they represent an advantageous jumping of two stages, as Beaton and Maddox have pointed out.[21] Even with Skybolt added, the V-bombers and their American equivalents the B-52s would have been obsolescent by the early 1970s, which was one of the reasons why McNamara cancelled Skybolt: the substitution of Polaris meant that a decision that would have had in any case to be taken about 1967 was taken in 1963 instead. The British decision to opt for Skybolt rather than Polaris when the choice between the two was originally offered by Eisenhower in 1960 represented consideration for the resources already tied up in the V-bombers rather than conviction as to the long-term value of the missile.

In view of all this, the press outcry in Britain against the reversed choice of Nassau seems rather surprising. Perhaps it owed something to a force active in the U.S. lobby against the scrapping of the weapon, the natural sense of grievance of airmen who saw their brief post-war ascendancy as the major arm of their respective countries' defence passing (in Britain) back to the navy or (in America) to the fixed hardened-site missiles which will provide most of the first-strike forces, and the navy whose submarines will provide the final reserve of second-strike power. Aside from this factor there was that of the pos-

[21] Beaton and Maddox, p. 28.

sible time-gap:[22] that the V-bombers without Skybolt may
be obsolescent by 1966, and Polaris will hardly be opera-
tional before 1968. The differential costs are strongly
favourable to a direct move to Polaris: as against the £350
million the submarine fleet is expected to cost, the probable cost of the V-bomber fleet with Skybolt for the rest of
its useful life was expected to be about £500 million, and
before the end of these costs had been reached the necessity of a move to Polaris at a further cost of £350 million
would have arisen. The cost of building the Polaris fleet,
£70 million a year for five years, represents only 4 per
cent of annual military budgets for that period.

It is possible to put the outcry over Nassau down to a
realistic understanding (not much put into words by
official persons, for obvious reasons) of its likely effect on
the negotiations with France, and British entry to EEC,
though it was perhaps the occasion rather than the cause
of the breakdown of the negotiations, because even if
Skybolt had survived Macmillan would certainly have
clung obdurately to the Atlantic rather than the Carolingian notion of Europe. The Nassau communiqué
offered Polaris also to France, ostensibly on equal terms
with Britain. But this offer was rather more diplomatic
than relevant: as de Gaulle said, 'It truly would not
be useful for [France] to buy Polaris missiles when we
have neither the submarines to launch them nor the warheads to arm them'. His preoccupation with the nature of
the Anglo-American connexion and its implication for
Europe is the central theme of the fatal press conference
of 14 January 1963. 'England is, in effect, insular, mari-

[22] Though the concern with a theoretical time-gap was somewhat unreal,
depending on an estimate of many unknowns, including the relative state of
defensive systems and the means to confuse them at the time concerned, a
matter which cannot really be tested except in war. The penalty for being
wrong is so great that a nuclear deterrent must become completely incredible
before it ceases to be effective. I owe this point to Brigadier W. K. Thompson.

time', he said. Moreover other states linked to Britain or to the free trade area would want to join the Common Market, and

in the end there would appear a colossal Atlantic Community under American dependence and leadership which would soon completely swallow up the European Community.... It is not at all what France wanted to do and what France is doing, which is a strictly European construction.

On the Nassau agreements he said:

the American nuclear power does not necessarily and im-mediately meet all the eventualities concerning Europe and France.... In this specific case, integration is something that is unimaginable.... It is quite true that the number of nuclear weapons with which we can equip ourselves will not equal, far from it, the mass of those of the two giants of today ... [but] the French atomic force, from the very beginning of its estab-lishment, will have the sombre and terrible capability of destroying in a few seconds millions and millions of men. This fact cannot fail to have at least some bearing on the intents of any possible aggressor.[23]

Inconvenient as de Gaulle's position may have been for Britain and America, one can hardly deny it some logical basis: As Kissinger has noted:

The issue of peace and war does not arise in terms of either-or. There are many intermediate stages where a country's bargaining position depends on the risks to which it can expose an aggressor. To some of our European allies it appears that even a small nuclear force is more effective for this bargaining purpose than a few more divisions ... our allies have an incentive to develop national nuclear forces not only to bargain with the Soviet Union but also to gain a greater influence over *our* actions.

[23] French Embassy, N.Y., 'President de Gaulle Holds Seventh Press Conference', 14 Jan. 1963.

Thus, for the dominant powers, restriction of the spread of nuclear weapons is a matter of the preservation of their respective power-positions and areas of choice. Again to quote Kissinger: 'The real basis of [American] opposition to national nuclear forces, then, is not so much their ineffectiveness as the fact that we do not want to be drawn into nuclear war against our will.'[24]

Incidentally, if the 'special relationship' between Britain and America had been merely the extension of nuclear-information privileges by America to Britain, the quasi-equal offer to France at Nassau might have seemed to end it, and was interpreted as doing so by part of the British press. But in fact the relationship has always had a quite different basis: it depends chiefly on the extension by Britain to America of a degree of determined assumption of common interest that has had no equivalent in the French relationship, certainly not in the relationship of de Gaulle's France to the U.S.

Since the end of the discussions at Brussels, American activity in the cause of avoiding the dangers of strategic dichotomy between herself and a Carolingian Europe has mostly been concerned with efforts to bring the multilateral mixed-manned NATO nuclear force into being. The absence of enthusiasm among the European powers, other than Germany, for this scheme has not been surprising. Congress had made it clear early in the development of the idea that there would be no further amendment of the McMahon Act to allow American atomic weapons out of American control through such an arrangement. This being so, the incentive for the European powers to undertake the considerable cost of a new nuclear force which would not have even the diplomatically-useful appearance of autonomy (since it would be as much under American veto as SAC itself) and which militarily could add nothing

[24] In *The Reporter*, 28 Mar. 1963, pp. 27 & 28.

to the American guarantee has necessarily remained slight. German readiness to co-operate has been with many sectors of non-German opinion a disadvantage rather than an advantage, giving the whole project the appearance, as Walter Lippmann said, of simply the 'easiest way to get Germany into the nuclear business'. And that prospect remains a danger to the delicate balance within Europe, as well as a danger to the hopes of *détente* with Russia. Harold Wilson said on his return from Moscow: 'The Russians make no distinction between Germany with nuclear arms at its full command and the mere share of the trigger which the American project involves.'

In reality the American proposals may only, as is said, allow Germany the appearance of a finger on the trigger while keeping a firm American hand on the safety-catch. If this is certain to remain the case the Russian apprehension may be ill founded but, surely, the German enthusiasm becomes surprising? One cannot altogether dismiss the thought that Russia and Germany may share a truer vision of the potentialities of the scheme than the State Department. But if America is determined on it as a sop to German sensibilities and a mode of undercutting any French bid to Germany in the nuclear field, then there is obviously a strong case for British participation, since predominantly Washington–Bonn developments are alarming elsewhere than in Moscow. The present division between the potential alternative governments in Britain in this general field of policy might prove the most important of any since 1947 in determining the future course of international politics. Certainly, for a new British government to refuse membership of the mixed-manned force while simultaneously cancelling the Polaris contracts on which the future of the autonomous British strike-force depends, and perhaps the TSR2 as well, would appear a programme ideally devised to ensure that West Germany becomes the most vital and influential of America's European allies, endowed with a potential veto on the further development of the Russian-American *détente*. For the Bonn government would become not only the provider of the lion's share of NATO's conventional forces on the Central Front (as it is already), but Washington's main partner in a force which would embody a large part of the West's medium-range nuclear-strike power, and this at a time when Britain's leverage *vis-à-vis* America would be decreasing anyway on account of the greater essential reliance on American power brought about by the loss of any British-controlled strategic nuclear force. It would be an act of irresponsibility, and not only to the British electorate, to choose to opt out of the mainstream of power without adequately weighing the fact that to do so is merely to resign one's place to those who may be not only less squeamish about power but less well served by the *détente*.

The inextricable connexion, for each of the dominant powers, between relations with the adversary and the diffusion of nuclear weapons among its own allies, was nicely underlined by the similarity of the situations of Kennedy and Khrushchev in mid-1963. Kennedy's somewhat abortive tour of his European allies in June, meeting recalcitrance over the mixed-manned scheme in Britain, and absence of enthusiasm in Italy, and conspicuously not meeting de Gaulle at all, had a certain symmetry with Khrushchev's dealings with the Chinese in Russia a week or two later. For both leaders it was a case of rather ambiguous chaffering with allies before an agreement with the enemy. The illustration is clear of how similar for the two dominant powers are the causes and results of the change in the central balance that seems likely to make 1964–9 so different a period from 1957–63.

The shadow condominium

A curious new element of 'self-fulfilling prophecy' has
been built into foreign-policy decisions in recent years. It
arises from the lead-time in weapons systems, that is the
time that elapses between making a decision about the
kind of defensive equipment that the barely prospective
future requires, and the actual embodiment of that decision in effectively operating military hardware. In the
larger fields of missiles or aircraft and nuclear weapons
this lead-time may be as long as ten years and can hardly
be less than five. It was almost ten years from the British
decision on atomic weapons and V-bombers in 1947–8 to
its period of full effectiveness as a strike-force from 1957–8,
and by that time the probability of this effectiveness ending seven years or so later, by 1965–6, was generally
acknowledged, and the necessity of making decisions about
its successor had to be contemplated. The mechanism
operates by the fact that since lead-time dictates that
decision-makers must contemplate the probable state of
affairs at least five years prospectively, and since foreign
policy is at present so much a function of defence neces-
sities, the choices made about defence at any particular
period embody themselves in a defence establishment five
years later, which in turn must tend to determine the
diplomatic alignments of that period. Thus the original
prophecy produces its own fulfilment.

Consequently what is now assumed (and assumptions
must be made) about the period 1964–9 will help create
the actual character of that period. This makes the deci-
sion-taker's responsibility a heavy burden indeed. But
quite aside from what policy decisions are now taken by
national leaders, certain factors are apparent about the
end of the 1960s, which already give it the look of a major
traffic junction in history. The heartrending extinction of

President Kennedy's life, a life which had been so hopeful for the world, has left the political prospects for America obscure not only as between Democrats and Republicans but as between the assorted contenders for the Republican nomination. Even if President Johnson obtains nomination and election in 1964, the uncertainty hanging over the prospects for 1968 will remain undiminished. For it is very likely to be a period of radical political re-alignment in America, since the race revolution at present rising to full fury there will certainly not leave the structure of American politics unchanged. Likewise, in the course of nature or of politics, it may well be the post-Khrushchev period in Russia. Since the impact of the conflict with China is even more unpredictable as to its ultimate results on Russian politics than the race revolution on American politics, both these landmarks in the world political scene are heavily mist-enshrouded. One knows they are there in the distance, but one does not know what their precise rugosities may be. As to the third major landmark, the fog is even thicker, and the crags it conceals may turn out to be grossly exaggerated—or, on the other hand, may not. For it is the prospect of China as in some degree a nuclear power. Since the revelation in August 1963 that Russian aid to China in the atomic field ended in 1959, estimates of the most probable year for this prospect have wavered. A Chinese official spokesman has said that China could not test atomic weapons for several years.[25] Yet recalling that Chinese work with atomic reactors has been in progress since 1957, and that Russia

[25] See statement by Chen Yi on 28 October 1963 that China intended to go ahead with plans for testing nuclear weapons 'but probably would not be ready for several years' (*The Times*, 29 Oct. 1963); also Beaton and Maddox, pp. 125 ff. and Alice Langley Hsieh, 'Communist China and Nuclear Force', in Rosecrance, ed., *The Dispersion of Nuclear Weapons* (1963). The author would like to acknowledge a general debt to Mr Leonard Beaton in this field, especially to his 'British Nuclear Independence' and 'A Nuclear Policy for Britain' in *Manchester Guardian Weekly*, 14 and 12 Feb. 1963.

under a similar incentive exploded her first atomic weapon just four years after the Americans had shown it could be done (thus confounding the intelligence estimates), one must be wary of assuming that China has no chance of doing the same in her turn. Obviously it would be a matter of the merest prudence for Chinese official spokesmen to refrain from optimistic forecasts until the eve of producing the first weapons, and for the pre-weapons-stage devices to be tested underground. There would be real dangers for a country in China's situation in being known to be on the eve of nuclear status.

The expiry of the North Atlantic treaty is also due in 1969, and presumably the question of its renewal or modification will before then have become a major issue. The France with which this question will have to be negotiated may well still be de Gaulle's France, and will have attained by then a considerable power of nuclear-strike. On the other hand, Germany might be Willy Brandt's Germany. These are, of course, only the central elements in the world power-balance. As to the peripheral elements, such as the position of India, prediction would require venturing on to limbs too fragile even for the present author.

All in all, there is no promise of its being a cosy period, and though it can hardly fail to be an interesting one, it offers to be so in the sense that reminds one that 'May you live in interesting times' is a traditional Chinese curse. This is the period for which decisions must be made now in terms of military hardware. And to make these decisions is to predict and limit the possible diplomatic roles for Britain over the period concerned. For, as was said, foreign policy today tends to be a function of defence posture. Probably this has always been the case for most countries: a few privileged ones, for instance Britain in the nineteenth century, and America for most of the time in which she was protected by the world balance, have enjoyed so large a margin of security that they managed to overlook the connexion. But no nation can do so today: the margin of power is too thin, even with the dominant powers, to disguise the structure that sustains it. One sees the skull beneath the skin.

Since the Cuba crisis, it has become more and more difficult to avoid viewing world politics in terms of what may be called the shadow condominium, and reactions to its emergence. 'Shadow' is here used in the sense in which one speaks of the Shadow Cabinet, or the shadow government of a society not yet fully sovereign. That is, the essential notion is of an alternative political order, waiting in the wings for its moment to take the stage. Perhaps not even content to stay in the wings: enacting something rather more like the scene in Henry IV when the prince tries on for size the crown he must inherit, before his dying father's eyes. The condominium in question is that of the two dominant powers, America and Russia, and its basic function is their joint management of the central power-balance. If one thinks of the essence of government as an effective decision-making process, with some will and some power to enforce decisions, one can see why the joint resolution of the Cuba crisis by America and Russia must look like the first interim operation of this shadow condominium. If government is, among other things, an enforceable relationship of command and obedience, Cuba was certainly under the joint government of the condomini in the final stages, in which the decisions were so clearly made over her head by the two dominant powers jointly. The condition for the condominium to come into being is a major crisis involving the interests of the dominant powers. And it only lasts for as long as the crisis: then it retreats into the shadows of the future, though not without leaving some signs of its passing. The chief such sign after the Cuba crisis was the establishment of the direct

teleprinter line between the White House and the Kremlin
—that is, a more efficient apparatus of communication,
negotiation, decision, for the condomini. The sense of how
strongly the President had felt the need of some such link
as the major lesson of the Cuba episode emerged clearly
from the television interview he gave at the end of 1962.

One may also regard the nuclear test-ban treaty as
evidence of the emergent condominium. As was said, the
condition for it to come into operation is the existence of
some factor involving the interests of the dominant powers.
And no question so closely involves their joint interest as
that of the access of other powers to advanced weapon
systems.[26] The reason why the test-ban agreement was
possible in 1963 when it had been sought in vain since 1957
was that in 1963 the interests of the dominant powers—in
the central field of their dominance—acquired a sudden
mutuality, because for both the question of rival and unpredictable powers became real. Nuclear tests do have,
or have had, a genuine role in the power contest between
America and Russia, in the search for an absolute lead in
weaponry. But in this particular field the rivalry between
the dominant powers had become less important to them
than their positions *vis-à-vis* other powers. No doubt they
also had technical reasons to conclude that a break-
through to decisive superiority was unlikely. But the
agreement has far more potentiality for freezing the *status
quo* as between nuclear and non-nuclear powers than for
freezing the *status quo* between the dominant powers themselves. That is why it was possible. Khrushchev's first joking
words to Harriman and Lord Hailsham, when they arrived
for the negotiations, 'Shall we sign the treaty right away?',
might be classed almost as Freudian-slip evidence of how

[26] John Strachey's last book, *On the Prevention of War*, though written
before these events, argues a case for the connexion between nuclear weapons
and the prospects for the emergence of a world state with great prophetic
insight.

much the agreement depended on the arguments he had just been through (with his Chinese allies), not the arguments he was about to enter.

This is not at all to say that the present diplomatic order is as yet on its deathbed, only that the power-balance is moving in a way that seems to augur its eventual demise. The present breakdown of the bilateral balance makes eventual new arrangements possible: it does not make them easy, and the transition will be agonizingly dangerous. That is to say, the central diplomatic problems of the foreseeable future are those affecting the potential condomini and their next rivals in power, in particular France (or 'great-power Europe') and China. There will also indubitably be plenty of peripheral diplomatic problems, stemming from local balances of power, as for instance between Indonesia and her neighbours or Israel and her neighbours. But if the central balance is adequately managed, local balances are unlikely in the nature of things to produce Armageddon. The first world war offers an example: the local balance in Balkans would not have produced it if the central balance had been adequately managed.

The limits on the ability of even the dominant powers, as yet, to impose their policy hopes on their alliance partners are well illustrated by a small sequel to the Cuba crisis. The natural elation of the President at this major success (very much a personal one: Kennedy himself made the decisions, even down to the question of which ships should take up positions where in the blockade) showed itself in a press conference at the end of the year, in which he reflected on the impossibility of sharing certain decisions with allies. These mild and entirely realistic reflections were simplified in the press reports into an alleged resolution to start bullying allies. What had not in fact been said had to be hastily un-said. Within a month there were illustrations, in de Gaulle's veto on British entry to EEC, and in the Canadian government's attitude on nuclear warheads, of how limited (except when the process is essentially one of tacit agreement between them as to their spheres of interest) were the powers of the potential condomini to decide even important policy lines for their closest allies. Jointly, they can decide the fate of the world: singly, neither can decide with any definiteness the fates even of Cuba or Albania.

This douche of cold water on any assumption that America's allies are readily manipulable provides a hint of the continuing usefulness to the process of diplomatic transition of Britain's role in the central power structure. Despite Dean Acheson, this role is not necessarily played out.[27] It is still that of 'Horatio, his friend' (even though the prince in this drama is rather more Henry V than Hamlet); that is, it is the role of a minor member, an 'attendant lord', with the oligarchs. The claim that by opting for this role Britain is sacrificing the chance to play other, more useful, ones is simply not realistic. The one usually suggested by those anxious to promote a change is that of 'leader of the non-aligned bloc'. But quite aside from the odd presumption that the major ex-imperial power would be acceptable in it, the world is full of states clamouring for this role, many of them with leaders at least as fluent as Canon Collins in the enunciation of the moral platitudes in which the part mostly consists. Britain's place is hardly among the diplomatic *ingénues*: it is in the

[27] Acheson's speech, early in December, must be interpreted as among other things evidence of his sense that Britain needed some urging to take the plunge, as far as Europe was concerned. He was rather more severe with the French a month or two later. The comments that charged him with Anglophobia were as baseless as the American ones earlier in his career that alleged Anglophilia. Like all good Secretaries of State, he has been interested primarily in the conservation of America's power and ability to make its own decisions. What chiefly distinguishes him from other American spokesmen on foreign affairs at present is his assumption of an elder-statesmanly bluntness.

backroom where the bargains are worked out. If one is old in diplomatic wickedness, the least one can do is to put the relevant experience to constructive use. The 'founder-of-the-non-nuclear-club' role is really a variant of the 'leader-of-the-non-aligned-powers' notion. There was a time when it was a conceivably useful idea, but recent events have made it irrelevant. Since the signing of the test-ban agreement it has become clear that it is the con-domini who will decide, essentially, who will be allowed to become members of the nuclear club. In any case, real economic and political factors make it unlikely that any nations other than France and China will make a bid for a serious power of nuclear strike. And it is unlikely that the plans of Mao Tse-tung or President de Gaulle would be affected by a British renunciation of nuclear power. For a time, again, the role of 'leader and voice of Europe' seemed to be open, but the present incumbent has made it clear that he tolerates no potential rival. Besides, in that joint household the motto is 'forsaking all others, cleave prim-arily to one's fellow members', and Britain was not able to take that vow in good earnest.

On the other hand, there are no other immediately eligible applicants for a place with the oligarchs, except China and a 'great-power Europe' which must reflect the dominance of France and/or Germany. It does not seem unduly nationalistic to assert that the influence of Britain on the management of the central power-balance should prove at least as reasonable and astute as that of either the other two potential members of the oligarchy. And since all our lives depend on the careful management of the balance, the diplomatic task of helping with it, even in a subsidiary way, is hardly one to be refused. It must, of course, be in a subsidiary way, essentially lending a little extra strength to America's elbow rather than as an inde-pendent agent. But the very limitations of British power,

which prevent her being a serious rival to the potential
condomini, make it reasonably acceptable to them as a
marginal weight in the system, more acceptable than a
'great-power Europe' or China which *are* potential rivals.
Britain is in no sense a revisionist power *vis-à-vis* Russia,
and one of the benefits of the stony want of British sympathy for Germany's very real grievances is that it exempts
Britain from Russian suspicions that she will endeavour to
pull German chestnuts out of the fire. As to America, the
intellectual as well as the diplomatic connexion can be
relevant in the next period. What awaits America in the
coming decades, in the way of managing the balance and
conserving coalitions, is an experience comparatively new
to her and comparatively familiar, on the smaller European scale, to Britain. The American nineteenth-century
experience was primarily of dealing with very much
weaker neighbours: Indians, Mexicans, Latin Americans
generally, Spaniards, Filipinos, Japanese, and Chinese.
The Utopian and moralistic foreign policy approach of
the early twentieth century was a natural outcome. Only
since 1917 has America had the experience of dealing as
a rule with powers that had—at first—something like her
strength and rather more than her cunning, whereas
Britain has always dealt primarily in a world where her
opposite numbers were of roughly equal (or potentially
greater) strength, and certainly equal skill in stacking the
diplomatic cards. The British diplomatic traditions—
alliance-building, compromise, accommodation, balancing of interests, tolerance of spheres of power rather than
efforts at radical settlement—were equally the natural
outcome of a diplomatic situation in which British strength
could never be truly decisive. History is now imposing
this restriction of choices on America: her ascendancy for
the future must lie in balance, not hegemony. Her moment
of true pre-eminence in power was brief and unrecognized.

Of course, Britain has no adequate power base to sustain her position in the oligarchy: but then she never has had, in the post-war period, and has nevertheless managed to pull it off reasonably successfully. If one has managed to walk upon the water relatively well for eighteen years, it seems unreasonable and faint-hearted suddenly to assume that one can no longer do so. And the auspices are unmistakeably good at the moment for a continuation of her post-war role *vis-à-vis* both the dominant powers. For conditions appear set fair for perhaps several years of *détente* between America and Russia, and this is a situation in which Britain's relations with America become easiest. Certainly the main elements on which the *détente* is at the moment being built—the *status quo* in Central Europe and joint action towards the prevention of any further diffusion of nuclear power—tread on no British toes, whereas they do, obviously, tread on German and French ones. The probability of ambivalence in the American attitude to 'great-power Europe' is still very much obscured by the habits of thought of a past in which the potential dangers and frustrations for America from a breakdown in the bilateral balance were usually dismissed as shadow-boxing. They are not altogether so dismissed now. Even General Norstad remarked at the beginning of 1963:

As we look back over the last twelve years or more, it is evident that a major factor governing the policy of this country has been the weakness of Europe. But in the decade ahead our plans and our objectives as a nation will be shaped to a considerable extent by the *strength* of Europe.[28]

Differing interests and vulnerability in regard to nuclear weapons, plus rivalry over power leadership were what split the Sino-Soviet alliance. It would be rash indeed to assume that the very same factors, inescapably present in

[28] *Vital Speeches of the Day*, 17 Feb. 1963.

the Western alliance, will necessarily prove powerless to do anything of the sort as far as it is concerned, especially since President de Gaulle's policy is based on the assumption of no immediate threat from Russia, and the present mildness of the cold war climate maximizes his freedom of manoeuvre. The major preoccupation of American foreign policy must be to keep under control the power-balance with Russia, so that on the one hand no important ground is given, and on the other not too much friction is created. The Europe they must seek is the Europe that will make this possible. And here Britain's interests are identical with America's.

In the world outside Europe it is equally the case that the dawning *détente* between the dominant powers underlines the usefulness of the diplomatic division of labour which the Anglo-American alliance has often been able to arrange. As tension slackens with Russia, it is very nearly certain to increase with China. For one thing, Russia will have a considerable interest in seeing that it is so, and for another intransigence is likely to seem to offer better diplomatic prospects than mildness to the Chinese themselves. Conceivably, Britain may within the foreseeable future be the only one of the major powers still to have diplomatic relations with Peking. Both India and Russia, the two that now share this communication post with her, are potentially within sight of a diplomatic rupture. And in the particular spheres in which frictions with China are likeliest to come—Laos, Cambodia, Burma, Vietnam, the Indian border—Britain is well qualified to operate as diplomatic principal. Until China's interests grow to resemble those of the other dominant powers, a main task in the management of the central balance will be to prevent her frictions with her neighbours (and through them with America) from reaching the point of major warfare. If it becomes certain that China is no longer sheltered be-

neath the Russian 'nuclear umbrella', the danger that
preventive war against China before she acquires her own
nuclear unbrella might commend itself in certain quarters
may well become acute. But it would be a dangerously
over-simplified view of the central balance to assume that
Western interests will always lie with Russia rather than
China. The West has certainly no reason to pull Russian
chestnuts out of the fire *vis-à-vis* China, and must always
bear in mind that the mildness of Khrushchev's present
tone to itself is a corollary of Russia's power competition
with China. Undue aid in the subduing of that competition would merely reopen the opportunities for renewed
Russian intransigence towards the West. That is, if the
schism at the Communist end of the balance of power is to
have any chance of operating hopefully for the West, it
must be useful to keep open some lines to Peking, as well
as the President's line to Moscow, and only Britain is in a
position to operate in the former sphere. The Western
objective must be such an equilibrium as will advance the
prospects of peace and freedom, not the success of either
party in the Sino-Soviet schism. But if Britain is to be
present in this area in terms of diplomacy, she needs to be
so also in terms of power. The revival of the notion of the
Commonwealth, in South Asia and the Indian Ocean
area, as among other things a security alliance, could
enormously ease the difficulties of India, caught at the
moment between the perceived vulnerability of non-
alignment, and the moral difficulty of any formal or overt
adhesion to the American camp. Commonwealth arrangements require no treaty-signing or official eating of words;
only a certain deployment of power and resources, which
can be as useful for the already existing defence obliga-
tions to Malaysia, and for the soothing of Australian
alarms over Indonesia, as they would be for India itself.
Until 1963 it was difficult to envisage any such role for the

Commonwealth, even with American backing, since British military strength seemed likely to be too heavily committed in Europe for any significant portion of it to be deployed east of Suez. But the shutting of the European door in January 1963, combined with the general turn in the world balance which has created the *détente* in Europe and the probability that the rimlands of China will be the scene of the new frictions, have quite reversed this prospect. Besides, the breakdown of the Sino-Soviet alliance, accompanied as it has been by accusations of racialism on either side, leaves the Commonwealth as the only trans-racial arrangement of any importance in international politics. In a world in which the prospective lines of diplomatic conflict look perilously as if they could become those of colour solidarity, this fact alone would justify a new look at the Commonwealth as a potential security alliance round the Indian Ocean. When China does manage even an experimental atomic explosion, the impact on Indian defence policy must be profound, and India has a better moral claim on Britain than on America for countervailing protection. America cannot reasonably be expected to underwrite every balance in Asia, and in this particular situation the dangers and discomforts, as far as Britain is concerned, of accepting responsibility might be less than those that would arise from refusing it and letting it fall elsewhere.[29]

[29] Any development of policy in this direction must of course raise acute difficulties with Pakistan. But Pakistan would clearly be even more alarmed at the possible alternative means by which India might seek to assure her own safety against a nuclear-armed China, for instance by acquiring her own nuclear weapons, or by seeking alliance with America or even, conceivably, with Russia. A Commonwealth arrangement would surely have less distressing consequences than any of these? Moreover there are already three Commonwealth countries concerned with security arrangements in the Indian Ocean area, or the southern periphery of China—Britain, Australia, and New Zealand; two others, India and Malaysia, are in transitional periods in foreign policy, with non-alignment beginning to be seen as an inadequate answer to security problems. Some influential Indian opinion is already beginning to canvass the possibilities of the Commonwealth con-

To put the *détente* with Russia down to the movement of the central balance is not at all to discount its importance and usefulness. On the contrary, it is precisely *because* it has resulted from this change in power-relations that it is far more hopeful than the short-lived *détente* of 1955, which had no such real basis. The developing schism on the Western side of the balance is still ambiguous in its portents, and it is inevitable for the time being that a large part of American efforts should be devoted to preventing its further development. But if this should prove a lost cause (and even given a success for the mixed-manned force that may in the long run be the case), then the only reasonable resolution is to strive for the flexibility of the multilateral balance along with its uncertainties. The new balance could just conceivably make possible solutions for the two great problems that the bilateral balance had to leave for fifteen years unsolved: the division of Germany and the freedom of Eastern Europe. The bargain that Russia seemed willing to make in 1955, of reunification in return

nexion being developed as a sort of middle way between the perceived vulnerability of non-alignment in the former style, and the electoral difficulty of alliance with America, even if such an alliance were available, which is in present circumstances very doubtful. America has heavy and increasing military burdens in South Vietnam, and the State Department is said to have made it clear both to India and Britain that it did not envisage taking on more, and would be glad of the deployment of reasonably substantial British forces in the Indian Ocean area. Presumably Harold Wilson's statement that he was prepared to see 25 per cent of British military power deployed east of Suez reflected his appreciation of this point. Malaysia's non-alignment is verbal rather than real: her security *vis-à-vis* both Indonesia and China rests entirely on the military guarantee from Britain. In effect, as far as Malaysia is concerned, the arrangement here envisaged is already in force, and it is of course one of the merits of Commonwealth arrangements that they can be developed without formal treaties. Whatever justification there may be for Pakistani resentments of past Indian policy, it would be as unreasonable to allow her a veto on such a development as it would have been to allow her to veto the Western arms deliveries to India when the Chinese incursion into Assam was under way. Pakistan's present assumption that the only balance with which she need be concerned is that against India may not be permanent, and in a still more distant future there may be reasons from other quarters than China for Commonwealth security arrangements in the Indian Ocean or the Arabian Sea.

for American withdrawal from Europe, could never have been acceptable to the West while there was no alternate source of strength in Europe to the presence of American troops and (hence) the credibility of the American guarantee. But with an alternate source of strength in Carolingian Europe, it might be possible, provided that American power remained close at hand in Britain, that some such accommodation should be reached. At some future date the Anglo-American relation might bear the same connexion to European security that it did in 1948, of providing the essential bridgehead to link American power with a Continental grouping absorbed in its own problems and balances. Contemplating the potential shifts and changes in a system of four major units, with some developing elements of condominium in the position of the two greater, one can hardly doubt the usefulness of Britain as a marginal weight in the American scale.

If it is to sustain so heavy a burden, the link between Britain and America must be kept in good repair. But the modes of strengthening it are not necessarily those usually prescribed. In particular, the prevalent left-liberal orthodoxy in Britain that the abandonment of British nuclear weapons would conduce to this end has been inadequately examined. Harold Wilson's apparent assumption when he was in Washington that this was the case startled some of his State Department auditors. There are no doubt several strands of opinion within the Democratic administration on this matter, and it is true that official policy is strongly averse to the further proliferation of national nuclear forces. But America after all has lived with the British nuclear force since 1957–8 without finding it dangerous or embarrassing, and even McNamara's famous denunciation of national deterrents in June 1962 was modified by a codicil a few days later in which he said specifically that it was not the British force he was talking about. For as long

as it seemed feasible that de Gaulle could be dissuaded
from his present vision of Europe towards a more Atlantic
one, there was certainly a case for Britain's being prepared
to accept a loss of autonomy in this field if she would per-
suade France to do so. But that time, if it ever existed,
appears to be past. One must beware of assuming that the
problems of 1964–9 will be identical with those of 1958–63.
If the balance does move towards a multilateral configuration, Britain must be to some extent in competition with a
nuclear-armed Carolingian Europe as the main potential
American ally on this side of the Atlantic. Can anyone
seriously maintain that the British nuclear force would be
irrelevant, either diplomatically or militarily, in that
situation? If the present tendencies are reversed, and the
Western side of the balance remains a single entity, it will
be because some effective mode of Atlantic sharing of
nuclear forces has been devised, and in that case the
nuclear dowry, as it were, that the European powers bring
to the joint household will do much to determine their
influence.

The actual dangers to Anglo-American relations[30] arise
rather from diminutions in effective British power, even
when those diminutions stem from the pressures of American policy. There is an old American axiom that the relevant question in politics is 'But what have you done for me

---

[30] In the bouts of intellectual self-flagellation that seem to be the newest
version of *le vice anglais*, it is often assumed that the British lack of enthusiasm
for integration into Europe may be attributed to an anti-Americanism which
means that the country is headed straight for the neutralist wilderness as
well as for reduction to economic rags and beggary. Surely this view is as
ill founded in the first point as it clearly has been in the second? For quite
aside from the obvious fact that a great-power Europe *including Britain* would
be the only state organism able to rival in power America and Russia, and
thus the one precondition likely to make such a neutralist policy seem some
day feasible, it is perfectly clear, looking at the evolution of events, that at
least at the governmental level what inspired British reluctance to 'go into
Europe' was not suspicion of it as a device of American policy but, on the
contrary, aversion to the idea of the European connexion replacing the
connexion with America as the closest of Britain's diplomatic ties. There is,

lately?' Since international politics are far more Hobbesian
than the domestic variety, the relevant question in assessing an ally's influence at any moment tends to be, even
more dismayingly, 'But what can you do for (or to) me
now?' The brutal fact is that international politics is a
system based on gradations in the power to inflict injury,
either on foe or (by default) on ally. It would be gratifying
if Anglo-American relations could be exempted from this
generalization, if they could be held to have escaped from
the world of telegrams and anger into some realm where
this sort of account was not cast up. But to reason as if
this were already or altogether so, as if some sort of commonwealth relationship already existed (in the old sense
of commonwealth as a political community), can only be
damaging and dangerous to the true relation. There is a
special relationship, it is true, but not of that sort. There is
a special relationship between America and each of its
allies, in the sense that each fills a different niche in the
structure of the American security system. America has
more common interests, probably, with Britain than with
any of her other allies, but nevertheless she must weigh the
relationship in the same power scales as she does other
alliances. The only serious enemies in America now of
British influence on Western policy are on the right, that
is they are those who resent what they interpret as an
excessive British pressure in the direction of accommodation with Russia and China. And power is what the right

of course, a segment of opinion on the left which is suspicious of both America
and Europe, and which at periods like that of the Cuba crisis of October-
November 1962 can perhaps look as if it represented a threat to the alliance.
But this element in opinion is like the froth on espresso coffee: there is less to
it than meets the eye. If one is using national reactions to Cuba to prove a
sad falling away in Britain's attachment to the Atlantic alliance, in contrast
to the stout-heartedness of the French, one has some difficulty in explaining
away the fact that a few weeks after these events Britain took a step (at
Nassau) which bound her more closely than ever to the American alliance,
whereas France took one which has divided the alliance more than any
other move since 1949.

in America, as elsewhere, understands and respects. Since the sharpest danger in America to British influence is the section of opinion whose case against Britain represents her as just a parasitic 'free-loader' on American power, less valuable and less worth listening to as an ally than sturdy power-oriented types in France or staunchly anti-Russian democrats in West Germany, it follows that every British policy decision that reduces Britain's autonomous power, and enhances her strategic dependence on America, endangers her influence in the alliance.

The process is double-edged: there is not only the direct loss but a kind of secondary, built-in 'resentment potential', well illustrated in the case of Skybolt. No doubt the original decision in 1960 that the costs of further independent effort in long-range rocketry were too much for Britain was reasonable enough, and the later extinguishing of Skybolt in McNamara's pursuit of 'cost-effectiveness' ought logically to have been received in the understanding that if one wants to have one's nuclear cake without paying the full market price, one must expect some discomforts along with it. They may be irksome, but then mankind is never without some incommodity or other, as Hobbes reflects. Unfortunately, though, the electorate is not made up of philosophers, and unreasonable as it may be, the resentment generated by these frictions of dependence could become a danger to the alliance if they were multiplied by multiplying the points of dependence.

The case for British nuclear weapons has always been, essentially, that lack of them meant total diplomatic dependence on the U.S. This situation has not changed: all that has changed is the Labour Party's attitude to it, so that Harold Wilson could talk in 1963 of the U.S. as 'the real, natural and only custodian' of nuclear weapons for the West. Unfortunately John F. Kennedy was not permanently the American President. Even his most like-minded rival, Nelson Rockefeller, took a rather different view from that of Kennedy and McNamara on the potentialities of European nuclear power, and the 'outside chance' contender in the presidential field, Barry Goldwater, propounds a policy whose nearest rational parallel is Taft's notion of 'Fortress America'. If Britain had to sit out such a presidency, the ability to be occasionally intransigent which some measure of independent power confers would be valuable for more than her own survival. In assessing some present American arguments in this field, de Gaulle's observation that those who have a monopoly always consider it the best arrangement is not without a certain wry truth. Denis Healey once observed that a nation's diplomatic leverage depended essentially on its power to help a friend or hurt an enemy. That is no less valid for the foreseeable future than it has been for the past, and the assumption that control of the most awesome variety of power ever created has no relevance to it is a curious one. Political judgements are not always entirely rational: the aura of military power may be more important than that power itself.

After Kennedy

In the first shock-reaction to the murder of President Kennedy the world had a momentary glimpse of the possibility that the whole configuration of international politics for the immediate future might be disastrously altered. That this now appears so unlikely is a testimony to the strength of the institutional devices for political continuity among the Western powers. In fact the West experienced in a few months of 1963 the loss of three of its chief decision-makers—Kennedy, Macmillan, and Adenauer, all powerful and complex intelligences, who had done much to shape events—and only in the case of the longest expected of these changes, Adenauer's retirement, did there seem much prospect that the policies identified with the man concerned might begin to die with the end of his tenure of power.

In Kennedy's death the loss the world sustained was not primarily a matter of the final year of his existing term of office. That would have had to be devoted largely to mending Democratic fences for him as it is for President Johnson. The momentum of the foreign policies already in operation will serve until the election, most of the advisers will remain the same until then, and in any case 1964 appeared a year likely to be as preoccupied for Russia with agriculture and other economic problems as for the West with political choices.

The real loss to the world was the Kennedy second term, which had appeared almost certain, and in which, as far as foreign policy was concerned, he would have been able to play a much stronger hand, take much more radical initiatives, than in his first term. The same advantages will not attend the man now to be elected in 1964. His relationships to the electorate, to his party, and to his allies will all inevitably be different. The emotion produced by the circumstances of President Johnson's accession to office may well stand him in good stead as regards nomination and perhaps election. But a new term for him could not be a continuation of Kennedy's undertakings in the way the remainder of the present one is. It must be an expression of his own personality and views. And Johnson appears a man of orthodoxy rather than innovation in foreign affairs. He was not one of Kennedy's closer intellectual collaborators in this field, nor has it been his own major interest, whereas Kennedy's personal dominance here has had only a few parallels in American history, chiefly Wilson and the two Roosevelts. It would not be surprising to see a reversion to the more usual situation in which the Secretary of State is the main policy-maker, as with Eisenhower and Truman. Though this need not necessarily mean any regression from the point Kennedy had reached with regard to the cold war, the process of breaking new ground may be slowed up, for this is a task requiring a sort of ascendancy over the Congress and his allies not readily or rapidly acquired by either a President or a Secretary of State. The hold that Kennedy had gained over the European imagination, which was important in keeping the dissensions within the Western alliance below danger-point, and which helped to ensure that the Atlantic concept of Europe's future looked more attractive than the Carolingian one to most European opinion-leaders, was very much a personal achievement. A President whose intellectual style is less cosmopolitan, more specifically American, may have a harder task. Moreover, the rapprochement with Russia was undoubtedly based in part on a kind of understanding between Kennedy and Khrushchev, duellists who had taken the measure of each other's steel. In a phase of world politics in which so much depends, not only on an assessment of the other side's intentions but on some assurance that the other side understands the nature of ones *own* intentions, the growth of familiarity of this sort seems a necessary preliminary to substantive change. Above all, Kennedy's large-minded imaginative understanding of the nature of power, the blend of caution and daring, judgement and intuition with which he used it was a rare enough talent. It would be expecting too much of good fortune for it to prove equally developed in the man who inherits responsibility in 1964, whoever that may be.

But when all this is said the fact remains that the historical process has its own cunning and that the intricacies of relations in the central balance depend chiefly on objective elements of national interest, which do not change much with the succession of new decision-makers. Since he has not inherited all Kennedy's advantages with his allies, Johnson is likely to work all the harder to keep the alliance viable. In the present phase of the struggle with France over the destiny of Europe, West Germany is the pivotal American ally, and was therefore likely to be the most assiduously cherished and cossetted, whichever President was in power. Fortunately this may not mean in Dr Erhard's time as restrictive an influence on the development of the *détente* with Russia as it would have done in Dr Adenauer's time. As to the relation with Britain, it will be largely conditioned, as it usually has been, by the two countries' respective functions in the mechanism of the world balance. Of all the sectors of European political leadership, Labour Party policy-makers in Britain were perhaps the most visibly influenced in their attitudes to America by the personality of President Kennedy. As Patrick Gordon-Walker put it, he was the man they trusted to hold the thunderbolt. There can have been few more cruel illustrations than the tragedy at Dallas of the dangers of basing a policy on anything so fragile as human flesh.

This essay has confined itself to considering the Anglo-American relationship as an element in the central power-balance, because the author would maintain that the failure to see it in this context is what leads to its either being sentimentalized or (and this comes to much the same thing) being written down as of no account. But to point out its relevance in the world of power politics is not to deny that this examinable diplomatic superstructure has its foundation in a less readily mapped historical and intellectual bedrock. No attempt at definition has been intended, only a contribution to argument. It is said that those from the outer provinces of polity often feel a stronger sense of its reality and extent than those from the centre. Perhaps it is therefore natural that the citizens of those distant and vulnerable provinces of the English-speaking world, Australia and New Zealand, should have a wistful sense of it as a diplomatic category, not merely a linguistic or sentimental one. The most notable other adherent of this viewpoint is President de Gaulle, though he maintains that misconception about Anglo-Saxons.